CAREER

DISCOVERY

ENCYCLOPEDIA

VOLUME 6
Ser–Z

FERGUSON PUBLISHING COMPANY
Chicago

Library of Congress Cataloging-in-Publication

Career discovery encyclopedia.

  Summary: Includes 504 articles on all categories of occupations with such information as description of the job, earnings, educational and training requirements, and other pertinent facts.
    1. Vocational guidance—Dictionaries—Juvenile literature. [1. Vocational guidance—Dictionaries].
I. Primm, E. Russell, 1958–

HF5381.2.C37   1990   331.7′02′03   89-26000
ISBN 0-89434-106-5 (v. 1)

Copyright © 1990 by J. G. Ferguson Publishing Company

All Rights Reserved

Manufactured in the United States of America
M-11

Editorial Staff

E. Russell Primm III
Editor-in-Chief

Susan Ashby, Sue Clinton, Alice Flanagan, Ann Heinrichs, Jim LiSacchi, Rena Moran, John Morse, Susan Sinnott, Mark Toch
Writers

Janice DelNegro, Chicago Public Library
Ed Gerler, North Carolina State University
Editorial Consultants

C. J. Summerfield
Editor

Earl R. Dale, Betty Dennis, Page Phillips, Jeannette Rattenbury, Linda Suzanne
Editorial Assistants

Carol Parden
Photo Editor

Shawn M. Biner
Text Design

Ron Villani
Cover Design

Carol Nielsen
Indexer

The Wordsmiths
Proofreading

Tom Myles
Production Manager

Contents

Volume 6

Key to Symbols 7

Secondary School Teachers 8

Secretaries 10

Security Consultants 12

Security Guards 14

Semiconductor Technicians 16

Services Sales Representatives 18

Service Station Attendants 20

Sheet-Metal Workers 22

Shipping and Receiving Clerks 24

Shoe Industry Workers 26

Shoe Repairers 28

Silverware Industry Workers 30

Singers 32

Ski Lift Operators 34

Social Workers 36

Sociologists 38

Soil-Conservation Technicians 40

Soil Scientists 42

Sound-Recording Technicians 44

Sound Technicians 46

Speech-Language Pathologists 48

Sporting Goods Production Workers 50

Sports Coaches 52

Stage Production Workers 54

Stage Technicians 56

State Police Officers 58

Statistical Clerks 60

Stenographers 62

Stevedores 64

Stockbrokers 66

Stock Clerks 68

Structural-Steel Workers 70

Studio Technicians 72

Surgeons 74

Surgical Technicians 76

Surveying and Mapping Technicians 78

Surveyors 80

Swimming-Pool Servicers 82

Switchboard Operators 84

Systems Analysts 86

Taxidermists 88

Taxi Drivers 90

Tax Preparers 92

Teacher Aides 94

Technical Writers 96

Telecommunications Technicians 98

Telemarketers 100

Telephone Installers and Repairers 102

Telephone Operators 104

Testing Technicians 106

Textile Technicians 108

Textile Workers 110

Tire Technicians 112

Title Searchers and Examiners 114

Tobacco Products Industry Workers 116

Toll Collectors 118

Tool and Die Makers 120

Tour Guides 122

Toxicologists 124

Toy Industry Workers 126

Traffic Agents and Clerks 128

Travel Agents 130

Truck Drivers 132

Typesetters 134

Typists 136

Umpires 138

Underwriters 140

Ushers 142

Vending-Machine Mechanics 144

Veterinarians 146

Video Technicians 148

Waiters and Waitresses 150

Watch Repairers 152

Water and Wastewater Treatment-Plant Operators 154

Welders 156

Wholesale Sales Workers 158

Winemakers 160

Wood Science and Technology Careers 162

Word Processor Operators 164

Writers 166

X-Ray Technologists 168

Index to Occupational Groupings 170

Glossary 175

Photo Credits 178

Index 181

Key to Symbols

 Professional, Administrative, and Managerial Occupations Jobs that require much preparation and training and involve a high level of mental activity. These people must apply theory to solve practical problems. They often direct people who are working together to achieve specific goals.

 Clerical Occupations Jobs that involve keeping records and accounts, filing papers, handling correspondence and other kinds of communications, and performing other routine work in offices such as those in business, government, and education.

 Sales Occupations Jobs that involve selling goods, services, or property on a retail or wholesale basis, including jobs as agents or brokers. In addition to selling, people in sales occupations often provide sales-related services to customers and may plan what products to sell and how to sell them.

 Service Occupations Jobs that involve assisting people with personal needs or daily activities. Workers typically prepare and serve food in restaurants, maintain buildings, provide grooming and health care services, and such. Also, jobs that protect lives and property, such as those in law enforcement.

 Agricultural, Forestry, and Conservation Occupations Jobs that involve outdoor work and the use and maintenance of the natural environment. Activities related to farming, ranching, fishing, hunting animals, caring for parks and gardens, logging, and some mining operations are included.

 Processing Occupations Jobs that involve purifying, blending, treating, or working with a wide range of materials, from foods to industrial products like paper or paint. To prepare these materials, workers use such equipment as vats, ovens, furnaces, mixers, grinders, filters, and molders.

 Machines Trades Occupations Jobs that involve operating machines to cut, shape, and work materials such as metals, plastics, wood, paper, and stone. Some jobs require being familiar with the details of how the machines work, reading blueprints, and making computations for adjusting machine functions.

 Bench Work Occupations Jobs that involve using hand tools and machines mounted on a bench or table in a workshop. Workers make or repair small products such as jewelry, clothes, shoes, instruments, or lenses. They cut pieces to size, fit parts together, and inspect finished items.

 Structural Work Occupations Jobs, usually outdoors, in constructing or repairing bridges, roads, buildings; installing telephone or communications equipment; or assembling structures. Also, jobs on factory production lines constructing motor vehicles, boilers, or large machines and equipment.

Secondary School Teachers

Other Articles to Look At:

▶ **Elementary School Teachers**
▶ **Guidance Counselors**
▶ **Librarians**
▶ **School Administrators**
▶ **Teacher Aides**

What secondary school teachers do

Secondary school teachers instruct junior and senior high-school students. They often specialize in a specific subject, such as English, mathematics, biology, or history but may also teach several subjects. In addition to classroom instruction, these teachers also plan lessons, prepare tests, grade papers, prepare report cards, meet with parents, and supervise other activities. Teachers often meet individually with students to discuss homework assignments or academic or personal problems.

Teachers design classroom lessons to meet their students' needs and abilities. They may lecture on a particular subject (history, for example) or use films, photographs, readings, or other techniques to explain a topic. Teachers always interact with the students and answer questions to make sure the students understand the lessons. In order to reinforce the material learned in class, teachers will assign homework, give tests, and encourage other projects that help students develop an understanding of the material. For example,

science teachers supervise laboratory work where students get "hands-on" experience and vocational education teachers provide students with hands-on work with tools and building materials. Teachers must always maintain classroom discipline.

Some secondary school teachers are specially trained to work with students who are mentally retarded or have other disabilities. Others work with very bright, or "gifted," students.

A teacher's day usually begins about 8 A.M. and finishes after 3 P.M. Before classes start, teachers take attendance and make announcements during a homeroom period. In between classes, they often oversee study halls and supervise lunchroom activities. Teachers often use free time during the day to grade papers and keep records of each student's attendance and classroom progress. After classroom activities are over, teachers often attend school meetings or meet with parents or students. Teachers must also use this time to grade more papers and prepare the next day's lessons. Many times a teacher is involved with a student project such as the school newspaper that requires after-school participation.

Education and training

Secondary school teachers should be knowledgeable in their subjects and able to communicate with and motivate students. They should have a genuine enthusiasm for working with young people and be interested in helping them learn. Teachers should also be able to present lessons in a creative way. Patience, understanding, and the ability to answer questions (about schoolwork and other matters) are very important.

The best way to become a teacher is to get a bachelor's or master's degree while completing an approved teacher's training program. Many colleges and universities offer these programs in their education department. Students must take a number of courses in the subject they want to teach as well as a number of education courses covering teaching techniques and related subjects. Students must also spend several months teaching in a high school under the supervision of an experienced teacher. Upon completion of the program, students receive certification as secondary school teachers.

All teacher must be certified before beginning work and many school systems require additional qualifications. While working, teachers must often attend education conferences and summer workshops to further their training.

Earnings

The need for secondary school teachers should grow in the early 1990s but so should the number of people interested in pursuing a job in this field. Many people enjoy the challenge of working with students and the advantages of having summers off.

The average beginning salary is about $23,500 a year, with experienced teachers earning about $29,000 annually. Those in private schools often earn less than those in public schools. Many teachers have summer jobs to supplement their salaries.

▶ A secondary school teacher explains a science project to several students.

Ways of getting more information

A good way to find out if you would enjoy being a teacher is to observe your own teachers at work. Most teachers will be happy to discuss the advantages and disadvantages of the profession.

In addition, write to the following for more information:

▶ American Federation of Teachers
555 New Jersey Avenue, NW
Washington, DC 20001

▶ National Education Association
1201 16th Street, NW
Washington, DC 20036

Secretaries

Other Articles to Look At:

▶ **Computer Operators**
▶ **Legal Assistants**
▶ **Medical Record Administrators**
▶ **Receptionists**
▶ **Typists**

What secretaries do

Secretaries help offices run smoothly. They handle correspondence, schedule appointments, do typing and word processing, take dictation, make travel arrangements, keep records and files, and take care of many other details that are so important to a well-organized place of business.

The job duties of any secretary depend on a number of things: the kind of business that employs them, their own job training, and the number of other workers in the firm who can do special jobs. Special jobs might include using shorthand and shorthand machines, working with computers, or dealing with foreign-language materials. Generally, secretaries employed in large firms do not do as many different jobs as those who work in smaller companies.

Many secretaries, however, do specialize. Some of the specialties include: *Legal secretaries* who prepare legal papers such as wills, leases, and court motions; and *medical secretaries,* who must be familiar enough with medical terms to be able to transcribe them from tape recordings. Similarly, *technical secretaries,* who work for engineers and scientists, must help prepare very technical articles and reports. These papers often include mathematics and graphics, which are very difficult to type into manuscript form.

Other kinds of secretaries include *social secretaries,* who work for a celebrity or high-level executive and perform such duties as arranging dinners and social gatherings, keeping an appointment schedule, and handling correspondence. *School secretaries* take care of the clerical duties at various kinds of schools, and *membership secretaries* work for associations or clubs, putting together membership lists and directories.

Education and training

Secretaries need a high-school education and some advanced training as well. Some students take business education classes, which include typing, shorthand, and business English. They then either go into the job market or enter college. Employers prefer hiring students who have had some technical training after high school, especially in the use of computers.

Still, most clerical workers receive some on-the-job training by the firm that hires them. There are many similarities among secretarial jobs, but many differences, too. Every business has its own way of doing things.

In general, secretaries need good reading, spelling, grammatical, and mathematical

▶ Checking the original document against the entry on the computer, a secretary maintains a computer file system for her director.

skills. Many companies give exams to job applicants that test these skills. Employers also look for speed, accuracy, and neatness. Careless mistakes are very costly for any business.

Earnings

The job outlook for secretaries is mixed. New computerized office equipment means that secretarial work will be done faster by fewer people. Still, companies are always looking for bright, enthusiastic secretaries.

The average yearly salaries for secretaries in small companies is $18,000. Secretaries who work in large companies earn about $20,000, with executive secretaries earning nearly $25,000.

Ways of getting more information

Students can get good job experience by working part-time as file clerks, typists, or receptionists.

For more information write to:

▶ Association of Independent Colleges and Schools
One Dupont Circle, NW, Suite 350
Washington, DC 20036

▶ National Association of Legal Secretaries (International)
2250 East 73rd Street, Suite 550
Tulsa, OK 74136

11

Security Consultants

Other Articles to Look At:

▶ **Bank Officers and Managers**
▶ **Crime Lab Technologists**
▶ **Police Officers**
▶ **Private Investigators**
▶ **Security Guards**

What security consultants do

A *security consultant* is engaged in protective service work. Anywhere there are important people or valuable property and information, a consultant may be called in to develop security plans as a means of protection. They are involved in preventing theft, vandalism, fraud, kidnapping, and other crimes.

Consultants often work with companies to help them protect their equipment and records from unwanted intruders. A consultant will study the physical conditions of a facility and observe how a company conducts its operations before making any suggestions. The consultant will then discuss options with company officials. The amount of money that can be spent on security will greatly influence the security proposal. For example, a large company that produces military equipment may fence off its property and place electronic surveillance equipment at several points along the fence. The company may also install closed circuit television cameras and hire several security guards to monitor restricted areas. A smaller company that makes com-

puters may only be able to install burglar alarms around specially restricted areas. A consultant will analyze all the possibilities and then present a written proposal to management officials for approval.

Consultants also oversee the installation of the equipment, make sure it is working properly, and then check frequently with the client to make sure the client is satisfied. In the case of a crime, the consultant must investigate the cause of the problem (usually working alongside police officers and other security personnel) and then adapt the security system so that similar problems are not repeated.

Security consultants may also be called on to protect famous people from kidnapping or other harm. These consultants accompany their clients on trips and conduct background checks on people who meet their clients.

Education and training

The work may involve a lot of travel, especially if the client is located in another city. Consultants should be in good physical condition because of the pressure involved in working on important projects, but great physical strength is not required.

The best way to become a security consultant is to combine several years of experience in crime prevention either as a police officer or private investigator with a college degree in business administration, criminal justice, or similar field. Specific training in an area of specialization is also helpful. For ex-

▶ A security consultant explains the best security system and its cost to business clients.

ample, if a consultant works closely with nuclear power plants, the consultant should have some previous work experience at a power plant and have a comprehensive knowledge of how these plants operate.

Earnings

As concerns for security continue to rise, consultants should find very good job opportunities in the early 1990s.

Earnings vary greatly depending on the consultant's training and experience. Those with a bachelor's degree can expect to earn $26,000 to $32,000 per year, while those with a master's degree should earn between $34,000 and $41,000 annually. Experienced consultants can earn over $50,000 a year.

Ways of getting more information
For more information write to:

▶ American Society for Industrial Security
  1655 North Fort Myer Drive
  Arlington, VA 22209

▶ International Association of Security Services
  PO Box 8202
  Northfield, IL 60093

Security Guards

Other Articles to Look At:

▶ **Police Officers**
▶ **Security Consultants**
▶ **State Police Officers**

What security guards do

Security guards keep public and private property safe from harm. They guard against fire, theft, and property damage. Sports arenas, office buildings, banks, schools, and stores are just a few of the places that security guards protect.

Other names for the various kinds of security guards are *patroller, merchant patroller, bouncer, gate tender, armored-car guard,* and *airline security representative.* Most security guards wear uniforms. However, in situations where it is important for the guard to blend in with the general public, ordinary street clothes are worn. Some security guards work during the day, while others are hired for night guard duty. A security guard might be assigned to one spot, such as at a doorway, to answer people's questions, give directions, or keep possible troublemakers away. Other guards make rounds, or regular tours, of a building or its surrounding land to make sure the property is safe and secure.

Security guards may sign visitors in and out of a building, direct traffic at a concert, enforce no-smoking rules, or inspect packages coming into a building. Often they carry wal-kie-talkies so they can communicate with other guards. Those who are likely to encounter criminal activity in their work may also carry guns. Security guards may work indoors or outdoors, day or night, and may be standing much of the time. They may have to work in bad weather and may sometimes face dangerous situations.

Education and training

There are no special education requirements for security guards. Most employers like to hire guards who have at least a high-school education. A security guard should be healthy, alert, calm in emergencies, and able to follow directions. Good eyesight and hearing are important, too. People who have had military or police experience are often considered to be good candidates for security guard jobs. Some employers require their guards to fit certain age, height, and weight guidelines. They may ask applicants to take sight, hearing, or aptitude tests. For some security guard jobs, experience with firearms is required. Applicants for certain guard positions may have to pass a security check, assuring that they have never been guilty of a serious crime. Security guards who work for the federal government are required to have previous military service.

Earnings

There is expected to be a strong demand for security guards throughout the 1990s. This is partly because the crime rate is rising and partly because so many older security guards will be retiring.

Security guards in the early 1990s earned between $3.35 and $9.69 an hour, with an average hourly wage of about $5.25. The difference in wages depends on the guard's experience and on the type of employer. Security guards working for the federal government earned a starting salary of $12,000 to $14,000 a year. Earning for government guards averaged more than $16,000 per year.

Ways of getting more information

Because of the experience required, young people ordinarily cannot get part-time jobs as security guards. However, they can perform similar duties as lifeguards, school monitors, and safety patrol workers.

For more information write to:

▶ United States Private Security and Detective Association
   PO Box 6303
   Corpus Christi, TX 78466

▶ With several television monitors at his disposal, a security guard is able to keep track of many areas at once.

Semiconductor Technicians

Other Articles to Look At:

► **Electronics Technicians**
► **Electronics Test Technicians**
► **Integrated Circuit Technicians**
► **Printed-Circuit-Board Technicians**

What semiconductor technicians do

Semiconductor technicians work in research laboratories, carrying out a variety of tasks to assist engineering staff in developing new designs for semiconductor chips. These tiny chips, often smaller than a fingernail, contain many miniaturized electronic circuits and components, and they are used in many kinds of modern machines.

The base material of chips, which are also called "microchips," is a semiconductor, usually silicon. Semiconductors are materials with electrical properties somewhere between those of insulators and conductors. Because the circuits in chips are so small, the area of electronics concerned with chips and their circuitry is often called "microelectronics." Semiconductor technicians are also called *microelectronics technicians*.

Semiconductor technicians work on making samples of new kinds of chips and on making limited numbers of chips that have been custom-designed for special purposes. To do this, they must have a broad knowledge of electronic theory, and they need to be familiar with the operating principles of the equipment in the laboratory where they work. They also must know about the specifications that their company has established for the products they will make.

Working under the direction of engineers, the technicians operate a variety of processing machines. Most of this equipment is highly complex and specialized. Using the machines, they convert layout designs for electronic circuitry to patterns that can be put on thin slices of semiconductor material called "wafers." They clean, coat, bake, etch, and treat in other ways the wafer surface. They deposit layers of different materials on certain areas of the surface. At various stages in the processing they test the wafers to verify that they have gotten the intended results. They cut the processed wafers into individual chips, then assemble and mount chips into appropriate coverings.

Semiconductor technicians must also keep records about all the steps in the wafer processing operations and about the results of the tests they perform. They may assist engineers in analyzing this data and in preparing reports to describe and evaluate the new designs they have developed.

Education and training

Employers usually prefer to hire semiconductor technicians who are graduates of two-year post–high-school training programs such as those offered at junior and community colleges or technical institutes. A program in electrical engineering technology or electronics technology is probably the best preparation for work in this field. Because a semiconductor technician's job involves a range of duties, a training program should include a good theoretical foundation. It should also help the student develop skills in reading technical information and writing clear reports.

While in high school, students should take courses in mathematics through algebra and geometry, physical sciences, computers, electrical shop, and English.

Earnings

The future prospects for semiconductor technicians are not clear. Foreign competition in the semiconductor industry may hold back the level of production in this country. However, the demand for microchips appears to be unlimited, because of their efficiency, speed, and low cost when used in many different kinds of machines.

The earnings of semiconductor technicians vary depending on their level of experience, geographical location, and their employer. In general technicians make salaries in the $20,000 to $30,000 range, although some may earn more and a few less.

Ways of getting more information

Students who live in areas where there are companies that manufacture semiconductors may be able to arrange to talk with a technician working in a research and development department. Membership in an electronics club or building electronics kits may provide some useful experience. By reading current magazines that cover microelectronics and

▶ At several lab stations, semiconductor technicians carry out various phases of testing on semiconductors.

computers, students can find out about the changes that are constantly going on in this industry.

Students may also write for more information from the following organizations:

▶ Electronic Industries Association
  1722 I Street, NW
  Washington, DC 20006

▶ Electronic Industries Foundation
  1901 Pennsylvania Avenue, NW
  Washington, DC 20006

▶ Electronics Technicians Association,
  International
  604 North Jackson Street
  Greencastle, IN 46135

Services Sales Representatives

Other Articles to Look At:

▶ **Door-to-Door Sales Workers**
▶ **Manufacturers' Sales Representatives**
▶ **Real Estate Agents and Brokers**
▶ **Stockbrokers**
▶ **Telemarketers**

What services sales representatives do

Services sales representatives sell various services. They may work for any company that has services to sell. Examples include companies that sell telephone, detective, printing, advertising, cable television, and linen supply services. They may also work for companies selling educational, computer and data processing, burial, dry cleaning, shipping, car repair, and hotel services.

The services that individual sales representatives sell may be very different. But the methods they use have much in common. First, they learn as much as they can about the services offered by their company. Then, they make lists of possible customers. To do so, they use business and telephone directories. They ask current customers for the names of others who might be interested in their company's services.

After identifying possible customers, sales workers meet with them and explain how their company's services can meet the customer's needs. They answer any questions the customer may have and try to convince the customer to buy their company's services.

Sales representatives may not immediately make a sale. They may make another visit, as well as call and send letters to the customer. Once a sale has been made, these workers visit the customer to make sure that the services have met their needs. They also find out if more services are needed by their customers.

Keeping customers satisfied is an important part of this job. Services sales representatives get many of their new customers through their current customers. Also, when customers are happy, they usually continue to buy the company's services.

Education and training

Many employers prefer workers with a college degree in a field related to the services being sold. For example, companies that sell computer services may look for workers with as degree in computer science. Those that sell advertising services may want workers with a degree in advertising. Job seekers with only a high-school diploma may be hired if they have a proven sales record.

Many companies have training programs for their sales representatives. Workers learn about the company's services and about various sales methods. They may also attend special training sessions given by technical schools, colleges, and universities.

Earnings

The job outlook for services sales representatives is quite good through the early 1990s. This is because of the rapid increase in demand for services. Many representatives do not stay in their jobs for a long time. As these workers leave their jobs, more openings will be created.

In the early 1990s, services sales workers had average annual earnings of between $22,000 and $25,000. Some experienced workers earn more than $100,000 per year. Most sales representatives receive a salary, as well as commissions (a percentage of the amount of sales they make). Some are paid only a salary. Others work for commissions only. Some companies offer prizes and bonuses for workers who go beyond the company's sales goals.

Ways of getting more information

For more information about a career as a services sales representative write to the following:

▶ Sales and Marketing Executives International
   Statler Office Tower, No. 458
   Cleveland, OH 44115

▶ Maintaining contact with customers, a services sales representative meets with clients regularly to make sure that her service is working well.

Service Station Attendants

Other Articles to Look At:

▶ **Automobile Mechanics**
▶ **Automotive Technicians**
▶ **Diesel Mechanics**
▶ **Motorcycle Mechanics**
▶ **Petroleum Drilling Occupations**
▶ **Truck Drivers**

What service stations attendants do

Service station attendants provide all kinds of services for the customers who drive into the gas stations where they work. They pump gas, clean windshields, and check water levels in radiators and batteries, oil levels in engines, and air pressure in tires. They may sell tires, batteries, light bulbs, and other parts; install accessories like windshield wipers, rearview mirrors, and spark plugs; and do minor repair and maintenance work—fix flat tires, replace mufflers, rotate tires, and add oil, water, and air as needed.

Some attendants drive tow trucks to stranded motorists and provide directions to lost motorists; others offer car washes along with gas tank fill-ups. In some stations attendants are responsible for keeping service areas and restrooms clean, for setting up displays, and for taking inventory of station supplies. In other self-service stations, attendants may only accept payment for fuel sold. Wherever they work, service station attendants must enjoy working both with cars and with the public, and must not mind the grease, grime, and long hours that go along with the job.

Education and training

It is possible to become a service station attendant without completing high school, but most employers prefer high-school graduates. Though applicants are generally trained on the job, some large oil companies have their own training programs that range from two weeks to two months—and for these programs a high-school diploma is required.

Training programs for service station attendants are also available through the distributive education programs available in many high schools. People interested in becoming mechanic-attendants should look into the programs with an emphasis on mechanics conducted by vocational education agencies and local offices of the U.S. Employment Service.

With experience and, in some cases, additional training, service station attendants can go on to become mechanics, station managers, or oil company salespersons. Many of the most ambitious and competent attendants eventually go on to lease a station from an oil company or buy their own service station.

Earnings

A moderate increase in the number of service station attendants needed is expected through the next decade. More and more Americans are driving cars every year, and, in addition to traditional services offered, more attendants will be needed to service the complex new pollution control devices on new cars. Off-setting this increase, however, will be the increase in self-service gas stations, where attendants are only needed to accept payment for the gas customers pump themselves.

Wages for service station attendants vary depending on the size, nature, and location of the service stations for which they work. Salaries are not high, however, with the majority of attendants earning between $7,000 and $12,000 in the early 1990s.

Ways of getting more information

Interested students can help parents pump gas at self-service stations, and can learn such routine maintenance tasks as changing oil, replacing windshield wipers, and fixing flat tires. Talk to the attendants at your local gas station for a firsthand account of what the job is like.

For more information, write to:

▶ American Petroleum Institute
1220 L Street, NW
Washington, DC 20005

▶ A service station attendant pumps gas for a customer.

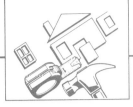

Sheet-Metal Workers

Other Articles to Look At:

▶ **Construction Workers**
▶ **Floor Covering Installers**
▶ **Heating and Cooling Mechanics**
▶ **Lathers**
▶ **Plumbers**

What sheet-metal workers do

Sheet-metal workers make, install, and repair rain gutters, outdoor signs, and other articles of light sheet-metal, including air-conditioning, heating, and ventilation duct systems. (Ducts are the long, metal tubes in buildings that carry hot and cold air or water.) Workers cut, bend, shape, and fasten the sheet-metal to form the desired object. Sheet-metal workers are often employed to work on homes and other types of construction projects.

When making an object, sheet-metal workers first determine the size and type of sheet-metal to use. Working from blueprints, drawings, or instructions from supervisors, they determine the measurements and angles of the object to be made. They then lay out the sheet-metal and mark the pattern to be cut. In many shops, workers use computerized measuring equipment to lay out the pattern so that the least amount of metal is wasted when the patten is cut. In shops without this equipment, workers use tapes, rulers, and other devices to make the measurements. Workers then use machine tools to cut the objects.

Sheet-metal workers do not make ducts or other objects from one piece of material. Rather, they measure and cut a number of metal pieces and then join them together to form larger sections of the finished product. Before the many pieces are joined together, workers must inspect each piece to make sure it is made correctly. They then drill or punch holes into the metal and assemble the parts by welding or fastening them together.

At the construction site, workers install ducts, pipes, and other objects by joining the various parts together and securing the sections in the correct location. Workers may use hammers, pliers, or other tools to make adjustments to the objects or make some parts by hand.

Education and training

Sheet-metal workers should be able to read blueprints and sketches and carefully follow instructions. They must be good at working with sheet-metal and using the proper methods for fastening metal pieces together. Workers need to be skillful in using handtools, power tools, and measuring devices.

The work involves a great deal of moving around, such as kneeling, reaching, bending, and stretching. In addition, the job may be physically demanding, requiring the lifting of heavy pieces of sheet-metal.

The best way to become a sheet-metal worker is to complete a four or five year apprenticeship program, which includes on-the-job training and classroom instruction. While under the supervision of experienced workers, apprentices learn to measure, cut, and install sheet-metal articles. In the classroom, apprentices learn how to lay out sheet-metal and read blueprints. Most apprentices are high-school graduates.

Some people become sheet-metal workers without going through an apprenticeship program. They acquire their skills informally by working as helpers while they learn. Helpers begin with simple tasks and gradually take on more difficult assignments.

Earnings

With an expected increase in construction and the need to continually repair or replace duct systems, there should be good job opportunities in the early 1990s. Some workers may experience brief periods of unemployment if there is a slowdown in new construction.

The average annual salary is about $35,000 per year. Apprentices start off making about half this amount, but their pay is increased every six months, so that they are making nearly this amount by the end of their apprenticeship.

Ways of getting more information

A good way to find about being a sheet-metal worker is to take shop courses and work with sheet-metal. It is also possible to interview a sheet-metal worker and in that way learn more about the profession.

In addition, write to the following organizations and ask for information about being a sheet-metal worker:

▶ A sheet-metal worker attaches a ring of metal to a cylinder.

▶ Associated Builders and Contractors
  729 15th Street, NW
  Washington, DC 20005

▶ Sheet Metal and Air Conditioning
  Contractor's National Association
  PO Box 70
  Merrifield, VA 22116

Shipping and Receiving Clerks

Other Articles to Look At:

▶ **Bookkeeping Workers**
▶ **Industrial Traffic Managers**
▶ **Postal Clerks**
▶ **Stevedores**
▶ **Traffic Agents and Clerks**

What shipping and receiving clerks do

Shipping and receiving clerks make sure both that their company's products are shipped properly and that the products they receive from other companies arrive in good condition. Keeping good records of all shipments made and received is very important in this work. In large firms the shipping and receiving departments are separate, but in smaller companies one or two people handle both jobs.

Shipping clerks check to make sure an order has been filled out correctly before it is shipped. Some clerks wrap and pack the goods for shipment or tell others how this should be done. In some firms, clerks order the trucks needed for the shipment and supervise packing the goods on them. These clerks make sure the merchandise is being shipped the fastest yet least expensive way possible.

The work of receiving clerks is quite a bit like that of shipping clerks. When orders come in, clerks check them against the ship-ping invoices to make sure the entire order has been sent. They then check the merchandise to make sure it is in good condition. If any part of an order has been lost or damaged, the clerk is responsible for make a claim or for tracking down lost goods.

The duties of shipping and receiving clerks vary widely depending on the type of company they work for. Some other related jobs include: *ship runners* who find space for cargo on board ships; *car checkers* who make sure freight trains are complete when they arrive at the railroad yard and report missing or damaged cars; *checkers* at stockyards count livestock as they are loaded onto trucks; and *vault workers* receive, sort, and route sealed money bags at the vaults of armored cars.

Education and training

Employers prefer to hire shipping and receiving clerks who have finished high school. Students should take classes in such subjects as business, mathematics, bookkeeping, and typing. Clerks must be able to read well and have handwriting that others can read easily. In some shipping departments, clerks may be expected to help with loading and would therefore need to be strong and in good shape.

Training for these jobs often includes periods doing such work as filling orders or stocking shelves. These workers become familiar with clerical work and usually have an easy time becoming full-time shipping and receiving clerks.

▶ A shipping clerk checks off the number of boxes that will be sent out.

Because little special training is needed for these jobs, competition for them can be stiff, especially in an area where the unemployment rate is high. Also, the number of shipping and receiving clerks may decline in the early 1990s as more firms, especially large ones, rely on computers to make their businesses more efficient.

The average yearly salary for shipping and receiving clerks in the early 1990s was about $16,000 with some going as high as $26,000.

Ways of getting more information
Part-time, summer, and holiday jobs are often available in this field. If shipping and receiving

jobs are filled, similar work, such as in the stockroom, would also give students good experience.

For more information write to the following:

▶ American Society of Traffic and
Transportation
  PO Box 33095
  Louisville, KY 40232

▶ International Brotherhood of
Teamsters, Chauffeurs, Warehousemen
and Helpers of America
  25 Louisiana Avenue, NW
  Washington, DC 20001

Shoe Industry Workers

Other Articles to Look At:

▶ **Furniture Upholsterers**
▶ **Leather Tanning and Finishing Workers**
▶ **Shoe Repairers**
▶ **Textile Workers**

What shoe industry workers do

According to recent statistics the average American buys four or five pairs of shoes each year. These shoes are produced by workers in factories who operate more than 300 different machines.

Cutters arrange dies on leather hides. A die-cutting machine then stamps out the parts for several matching pairs of shoes. *Stock handlers* then take these cut parts to a fitting room where *fitting room workers* make the upper parts of the shoes. They use machines to punch holes in the uppers, trim cloth linings, taper edges, put in eyelets and buckles, and lace the shoes.

Meanwhile, workers in sole rooms are preparing insoles, outsoles, and heels. Workers take these parts to last rooms. A *last* is a wooden or plastic form shaped like a foot. Workers called *last assemblers* put the upper and lower parts of a shoe on a last, and then run machines that join the parts together.

The next stop is the bottoming department, where workers attach steel or wooden shanks and outsoles to the shoes. The shoes are then removed from the lasts and set to the finishing department.

Workers in the finishing department put heels on the shoes and trim the outsoles. They also cement cloth linings and inner heel pads in place. *Treeing* and *packing department workers* clean, finish, and polish the upper parts of the shoes. Finally, *packers* pack the shoes for storing or shipping.

Education and training

Although a high-school education is not required for consideration as a shoe industry worker, applicants with a diploma are likely to be hired before those who have not graduated. High-school courses that would be helpful include shop and sewing courses. Some technical schools offer courses in shoemaking. Students who complete such courses will probably start at a higher wage than those with no training.

Most shoe industry workers learn their skills on the job. It may take from six months to two years for workers to become highly skilled at their jobs.

Earnings

The employment opportunities for shoe industry workers in the early 1990s should be slower than average. Many shoes are now imported from foreign countries causing the need for fewer workers in the United States.

Most shoe industry workers are paid by piecework rates. This means they get paid

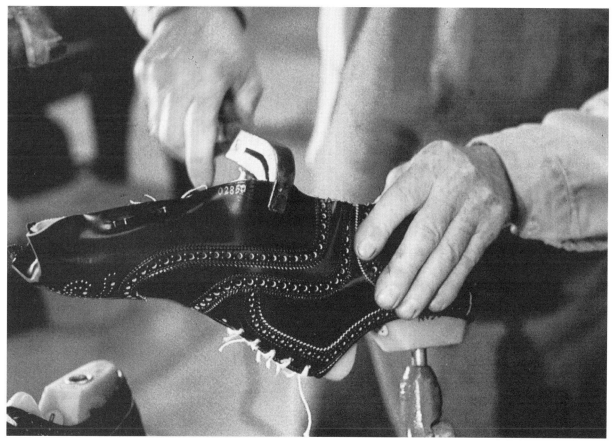

▶ Shaping the upper section of a leather shoe, a shoe industry worker prepares the shoe for sewing.

according to how much they produce. In the early 1990s the average pay for shoe industry workers was about $12,000 per year. The highest paid shoe industry workers are cutters, who average about $17,000 a year.

New workers usually start at the prevailing minimum wage. After they learn their skill they can work quickly enough to be paid a piecework rate.

Ways of getting more information

For more information about a career as a shoe industry worker, write to the following.

▶ Shoe Service Institute of America
5024-R Campbell Road
Baltimore, MD 21236

Shoe Repairers

Other Articles to Look At:

▶ **Dry Cleaning and Laundry Workers**
▶ **Leather Tanning and Finishing Workers**
▶ **Retail Sales Workers**
▶ **Retail Store Managers**
▶ **Textile Manufacturing Workers**

What shoe repairers do

Shoe repairers fix shoes, most often heels and soles, and they also work on such other leather products as purses, luggage, saddles, and harnesses. Some workers, often called *custom shoemakers,* design and make special orthopedic shoes, which are prescribed by podiatrist for persons with medical problems.

Most shoe repairers work in small shops where they perform the whole range of jobs, such as sewing, trimming, dying, polishing, and so on. Many other shoemakers own their shops and so must combine the skills of a small business person with those of a shoemaker. Besides fixing shoes, those workers make estimates of repair costs, write up sales slips, do basic bookkeeping and accounting, and often supervise other employees.

Shoe repairers may start out working with a small kit, cleaning, polishing, and doing minor repairs on leather in locations where business workers are likely to be found. Airports, bus stations, train stations, and other areas where people may have some spare time for getting their shoes polished are the most practical locations for shoe repairers.

A good shoe repairer must have the ability to work with precision and skill on small areas. In order to restitch a shoe, the worker should be able to either run a sewing machine or hand stitch an area along the same path it was originally sewn. Replacing worn soles or heels needs to be done so that the wearer can still feel comfortable in the shoes.

Dying shoes requires knowledge of dyes and how leather responds to the dyes. To match a dress color, the shoe repairer needs to know how dark the leather will get from the dye. Experience and testing are the most effective ways to learn the trade.

Working with specific leather items such as saddles may be done by people who choose to specialize in the crafting of one product, but since leather is used, any shoe repairer can add those items to his or her list of crafts. Purses, gloves, saddles, and other sewn leather products may require repair or restitching and if a shoe repairer is qualified to work on those things, it will increase the amount of business done.

Education and training

There are no special requirements for becoming a shoe repair worker, although a high-school diploma or vocational school training is helpful. Training programs are offered by the U.S. Government's Manpower Development and Training Act.

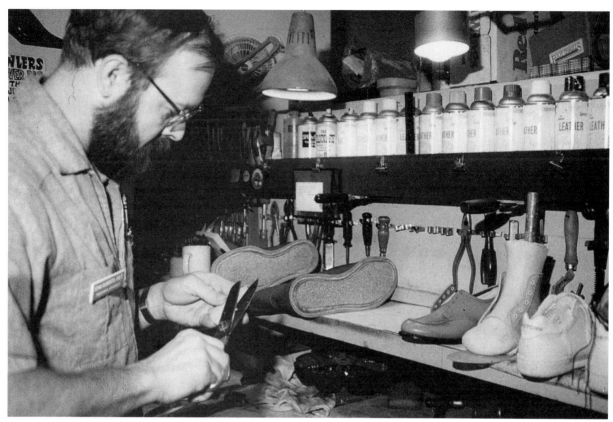

▶ A shoe repairer cuts a piece of leather to put on a shoe.

These workers should have good hand to eye coordination and good eyesight. Apprenticeship and studying under someone who has experience is the best way to learn the trade.

Earnings

The demand for shoe repair workers is decreasing somewhat in the early 1990s as more people wear shoes that don't need repair work—athletic shoes, for example. Leather is still a popular material, however, and mending should be in demand for some time to come. With quality leather it may be more important to the owner to keep that item in shape instead of replacing it. Favorite saddles, shoes, and purses will need repair with use and a skilled leather craftsman will find clients.

The average earning for shoe repair workers is between $13,000 and $18,000 per year, with shop owners earning quite a bit more.

Ways of getting more information

For more information write to:

▶ Shoe Service Institute of America
   5024-R Campbell Boulevard
   Baltimore, MD 21236

▶ Leather Industries of America
   2501 M Street, NW
   Washington, DC 20037

Silverware Industry Workers

Other Articles to Look At:

► **Designers**
► **Electroplating Workers**
► **Forge Shop Workers**
► **Glass Manufacturing Workers**
► **Jewelers and Jewelry Repairers**
► **Tool and Die Makers**

What silverware industry workers do

Silverware industry workers design and manufacture flatware and hollowware. Eating utensils such as forks, knives, and spoons are know as flatware. Containers such as pitchers, sugar bowls, and cups are know as hollowware. Flatware and hollowware can be made of a variety of materials. These include sterling silver, pewter, or stainless steel. Some flatware is plated, which means it has a coating of silver or gold over another metal. Hollowware may also be plated.

Silverware designers design flatware and hollowware. They make drawings of the pieces as well as the patterns (if any) that will go on them. After a design has been approved, *modelers* use clay or plaster to make a mold of the piece. This model is used by *tool and die makers* to make steel dies of the piece. These dies are used in cutting, shaping, and stamping the metal. Next, sheets of metal are fed into machines that cut them into flat shapes. These shapes are then formed and rounded by other machines. The extra metal is trimmed away by workers called *trimmers*. Rough edges are smoothed on a belt. Workers stamp designs on the handles of pieces. To do so, they use dies and a drop hammer. The pieces are then washed and polished. Polishing may involve holding each piece against a rotating wheel.

The spouts, handles, and other parts of plated hollowware are made by poring melted metal into molds. *Silverware assemblers* attach these parts to teapots, cream pitchers, and other types of hollowware. To do so, they use solder or another type of adhesive (glue). Then, the pieces are placed with silver, gold, or a mixture of metals. This is the job of *electroplaters. Oxidizers* place a solution on silver or silver-plated pieces. This solution makes the design stand out after the piece has been buffed.

Most silverware industry workers are employed by factories located in New England. Factories are also found in the state of New York and in other areas of the country.

Education and training

An associate's or bachelor's degree in design is usually needed to become a silverware designer. Skilled workers in this field must complete an apprenticeship program. These programs combine classroom work with on-the-job training. Workers who have completed technical school programs in related fields are in demand in this industry. Even those applying for unskilled jobs should have a high-school diploma, if possible.

▶ Using one spoon to compare to the following spoons, a silverware industry worker checks the curve of the handles against the original model.

Earnings

The job outlook for silverware industry workers is not very good. One reason is that more and more of the silverware being sold in this country is imported. The high price of silver and steel has also had a bad effect on this country. Most job openings will occur as workers switch to other fields or retire. Few new jobs will be created.

Salaries of silverware designers range from $15,000 per year to more than $20,000. Skilled workers who get paid by the piece may make more than $9.00 per hour. Unskilled workers start at about $5.50 to $7.00 per hour. Tool and die makers can earn as much as $12.00 per hour.

Ways of getting more information

For more information about careers in the silverware industry write to the following:

▶ Manufacturing Jewelers & Silversmiths of America
   The Biltmore Plaza Hotel
   Providence, RI 02903

▶ Sterling Silversmiths Guild of America
   312A Wyndhurst Avenue
   Baltimore, MD 21210

Singers

Other Articles to Look At:

▶ **Music Teachers**
▶ **Musicians**

What singers do

Singers are musicians whose instruments are their voices. Singers use their knowledge of musical tone, phrasing, harmony, and melody to create vocal music.

Singers are classified in two ways. They may be classified by the range of their voices. Sopranos have the highest voices, followed by contraltos, tenors, altos, and basses, who have the lowest voices. Singers may also be classified by the type of music they sing— rock, folk, classical, jazz, or country.

Nearly all singers work with instrumental musicians. A singer's backup group may be as small as a solitary piano player or a single guitarist or as large as a full symphony orchestra. In between are jazz combos, dance bands, rock bands, and so on.

Many singers travel throughout the country and even the world bringing their music to appreciative audiences. A jazz singer, for example, may play to audiences in small clubs in cities across the United States. An opera singer, by comparison, may sing in huge opera houses in the Americas, Europe, and on the other continents.

Some singers are primarily studio singers. That is, they rarely perform in front of audiences. Rather, they do their performing in sound studios. They may record television and radio commercials, jingles, and the like.

Singers can also be actors. Musical plays on the stage require singers with strong voices who can also act well. Many singers have made their careers in such plays.

Many singers choose to be teachers. Young singers need vocal training. Just as piano teachers help their students to master the keyboard, singing teachers help their students to master their vocal talents. Singing teachers help students learn to read music, develop their voices, and breathe correctly.

Education and training

Most singers begin learning their craft at an early age. Young children may be part of school or church choirs. In high school, students may join concert choirs or take part in musical plays that include extensive vocal training. Usually, students must audition for enrollment in these programs.

In addition to formal schooling, many singers enlist the aid of singing teachers and voice coaches. These teachers help their students to refine their vocal talents. No amount of training, however, can substitute for talent, dedication, and drive. Singers must be truly devoted to their craft to succeed.

Earnings

There always has been strong competition for the limited number of job opportunities for

▶ A cast of singers perform an operetta on stage.

singers. Only the most talented will find regular employment in the early 1990s.

Singers wages vary so widely that it is impossible to give a true indication of a vocalist's earning power. Singers, whether popular or classical, who become famous can expect to earn a good deal of money. Many studio singers also earn good wages. Some singers, however, are barely able to support themselves from their earnings and must work at other jobs to gain additional money.

Ways of getting more information

For more information about a career as a singer writing to the following:

▶ American Federation of Musicians of the U.S. and Canada
  Paramount Building
  1501 Broadway, Suite 600
  New York, NY 10036

▶ American Guild of Musical Artists
  1727 Broadway
  New York, NY 10019

▶ National Association of Schools of Music
  11250 Roger Bacon Drive, No. 21
  Reston, Va 22090

Ski Lift Operators

Other Articles to Look At:
- ▶ **Electrical Repairers**
- ▶ **Hotel and Motel Workers**
- ▶ **Operating Engineers**
- ▶ **Recreation Workers**
- ▶ **Structural Steel Workers**

What ski lift operators do

Ski lift operators maintain and run the lifts that carry skiers to the top of a slope. There are several types of ski lifts. With a rope tow, skiers grasp a motor-driven rope and are pulled uphill. The chair lift features a series of chairs that hang from a moving cable. Skiers sit on the chairs and are transported uphill. Gondolas and tram lifts operate like a chair lift but have enclosed cars to carry skiers to the top of the slope. Although ski lift operators maintain and operate all types of ski lifts, most work with chair lifts.

Ski lift operators work in resorts that feature downhill skiing. Operators must check the loading area around the ski lift to make sure it is clear of all freshly fallen snow, ice, or other material. The loading platform must be clear to allow skiers to get on and off as safely as possible. Operators then check the electrical equipment that powers the lift. They inspect the engine and observe the brakes, gearbox, and other parts. Operators might make minor adjustments to the equipment, but any major repairs are referred to the maintenance staff. The operators then turn on the ski lift and test it by having one of the operators ride the lift to the top of the slope. This operator must check the connecting cables and other equipment along the way. The brakes are also tested. Again, any repair problems are referred to the maintenance staff.

Throughout the day, operators at the bottom of the slope help skiers on the lift while those at the top help skiers off the lift. If someone is not seated properly or has trouble getting on or off the lift, the operator stops the lift until the problem is resolved.

Education and training

Ski lift operators usually have at least a high-school degree and some skiing experience. The skiing background helps operators relate to other skiers and makes them aware of possible problems skiers might have with the lifts. Many operators have at least some college training, and often operators are college students who are working part-time or taking time off from school.

All beginning ski lift operators are given on-the-job training under the supervision of experienced operators. New operators are shown how to maintain and run the equipment and how to help skiers in the most effective manner.

Earnings

Skiing and other outdoor sports are gaining in popularity and this should lead to good job op-

▶ A ski lift operator guides skiiers on to the chair lift.

portunities in the early 1990s for ski lift operators. Ski lift operators only work during the winter months (late November to April) and each year there are many openings to replace those who do not return from the previous season.

The average salary is about $8.00 an hour. Operators can expect to earn several thousand dollars during the winter months. Because the job is part-time, most operators do not receive health insurance, vacation, or other benefits.

Ways of getting more information
A good way to find out if you would enjoy being a ski lift operator is to visit a ski resort and talk to an operator. It might also be possible to get a part-time job as an operator's helper and in that way learn more about the profession.

In addition, write to the following organization and ask for information about being a ski lift operator:

▶ United States Ski Association
PO Box 100
Park City, UT 84060

Social Workers

Other Articles to Look At:

▶ **Career Counselors**
▶ **Guidance Counselors**
▶ **Human Services Workers**
▶ **Psychologists**
▶ **Rehabilitation Counselors**
▶ **Sociologists**

What social workers do

Social workers work with people to ease personal and community problems caused by such things as poverty, homelessness, unemployment, illness, broken homes, family discord, and physical, mental, and emotional handicaps. Employed by public and private agencies, social workers do their job through individual casework, group work, or community organizations.

In casework, the social worker, or caseworker, meets face-to-face with the troubled individual or family. These caseworkers may work in schools, to help students who skip school or have other behavior problems. They may work in hospitals, helping sick people and their families adjust to the special problems caused by their illnesses. They may work in courts, police departments, and prison systems, counseling convicts, helping juvenile offenders, or assisting soon-to-be released prisoners return to life outside the jail. Some caseworkers are employed by adoption agencies; some work in drug and alcohol abuse programs; some work privately to help families find solutions to financial, emotional, or medical problems. Whether they meet in their own offices, in the clients' homes, or in official settings like schools and hospitals, caseworkers do their best to help clients resolve whatever problems are troubling them.

Group workers may be employed by community centers, settlement houses, youth organizations, institutions for children or the aged, hospitals, prisons, or housing projects. They provide both rehabilitation and recreational activities for groups of people with similar handicaps or problems. Group workers might help migrant workers adjust to their temporary surroundings. They might hold workshops for parents of diabetic children or for the children themselves. They might work in nursing homes, planning social and recreational activities for the elderly. They often provide the same kinds of services that individual caseworkers do, only on a group basis.

Community organization workers try to analyze problems of an entire community, and to discover ways to solve them. Juvenile delinquency is one problem that might require total community cooperations for solution; high unemployment or crime rates are others.

Education and training

A social worker needs at least a bachelor's degree in social work from an approved four-year college or university. Jobs with the most rewards and responsibilities go to applicants with a master's degree. A doctorate is required for some teaching, research, and supervisory jobs.

Earnings

Overall job prospects for social workers should be better than average through the mid-1990s, though competition for the best jobs may be stiff. As always, workers with the best education and most experience will win the best jobs.

Beginning social workers with a bachelor's degree earned about $17,700 in the early 1990s. Those with a master's degree earned salaries ranging from $22,300 to $30,800, depending on their experience.

Ways of getting more information

Your library will have plenty of reading material on the history and nature of social work. For more direct information, contact a local social agency, hospital, or community organization that uses social workers in its programs. Volunteering as a junior counselor at a day camp will also offer opportunities to see what working with different sorts of people is like.

For more information write to:

▶ In a conference with clients, a social worker discusses the ways to handle the clients' problems.

▶ Council on Social Work Education
    1744 R Street, NW
    Washington, DC 20009

▶ National Association of Social Workers
    7981 Eastern Avenue
    Silver Spring, MD 20910

Sociologists

Other Articles to Look At:
- ► **Anthropologists**
- ► **College and University Faculty**
- ► **Economists**
- ► **Political Scientists**
- ► **Psychologists**
- ► **Social Workers**

What sociologists do

Sociologists study the various groups that human beings form. They study families, tribes, communities, and other social and political groups to understand how they develop and operate. To study these groups, sociologists observe them and record scientific information about what they find. Besides observing groups themselves, sociologists may use population counts, historical documents, questionnaires, and tests. Lawmakers, educators, and others then use this information to help solve social problems.

A sociologist can specialize in any of several fields. Criminologists study causes of crime and ways to prevent it. *Urban sociologists* study cities and the ways people live within them. *Industrial sociologists* specialize in the relationships between employees in company. *Clinical sociologists* study groups that do not work well or are poorly organized, and they help find ways to improve them. *Social ecologists* learn about how the environment affects where and how people live. These are just a few of the many areas in which sociologists may choose to work.

Sociologists often work closely with other social scientists and scientific professionals. For instance, statisticians help to organize the information they collect into mathematical formulas. They also work with psychologists, cultural anthropologists, economists, and political scientists.

Over two-thirds of all sociologists teach in colleges and universities. They may be working on sociology research projects at the same time. Other sociologists work for government agencies that deal with poverty, crime, community development, and similar social problems.

Education and training

With a bachelor's degree in sociology, a person can perhaps get a job doing interviews or collecting data. With a teaching certificate, he or she can teach sociology in a high school. Those with master's degrees can find jobs with research institutes, industries, or government agencies. It is important to note, however, that more than half of all working sociologists have a doctorate. Most of them teach in colleges and universities while doing their research. Helpful high-school courses include English, a foreign language, mathematics, sciences, social studies, and other college preparatory courses.

Sociologists who wish to work for the federal government may be required to take a civil service examination. Those who want to

▶ A group of sociologists discuss their findings from a group study.

work overseas may have to take a foreign-language proficiency test. Some clinical sociologists have to be certified by the Clinical Sociology Association (CSA). This requires a doctoral degree, one year's experience as a clinical sociologist, and other proof of knowledge and skills.

Earnings

Job opportunities for sociologists in the early 1990s will increase more slowly than average. The best jobs will go to those with doctoral degrees, while people with a master's degree will find themselves in stiff competition for jobs.

In the early 1990s, a sociologist with a bachelor's degree working for the federal government started at $14,400 to $17,800 a year. The starting salary for sociologists with

doctorates was around $26,400, although some started at $31,600. The middle salary level for sociologists working in industries was $45,000, and for those in universities it was $37,000.

Ways of getting more information

For more information write to:

▶ American Sociological Association
  1722 N Street, NW
  Washington, DC 20036

▶ Clinical Sociology Association
  2600 Timber Lane
  La Crosse, WI 54601

▶ Population Association of America
  1429 Duke Street
  Alexandria, VA 22314

Soil-Conservation Technicians

Other Articles to Look At:

▶ **Agricultural Engineers**
▶ **Agricultural Scientists**
▶ **Farm Crop Production Technicians**
▶ **Foresters**
▶ **Forestry Technicians**
▶ **Surveying and Mapping Technicians**

What soil-conservation technicians do

Soil-conservation technicians help land users to develop plans to use the soil wisely. They show farmers how to rotate their crops so that the nutrients in the soil are not exhausted. They also help foresters plan growth and harvesting cycles so that trees are not cut down faster than new ones can be planted and mature.

Soil-conservation technicians perform a variety of duties. They assist engineers in surveying land. They plan tile drainage systems and irrigation systems. Soil-conservation technicians also make maps from aerial photographs and inspect specific areas to determine what conservation methods are needed.

Experienced soil-conservation technicians have specific titles and jobs. *Cartographic technicians* are responsible for charting or mapping areas of the earth. They also create that show specific geographic information. *Geodetic technicians* help to analyze, evaluate,

compute, and select geodetic data—information that relates to the size, shape, and gravity of the earth. *Engineering technicians* test engineering materials for performance and efficiency, and write reports on their findings.

Meteorological technicians analyze or predict weather and its effect on the earth's surface and on the activities of people. *Physical science technicians* assist professional scientist in adjusting and operating measuring instruments, mixing solutions, making routine chemical analyses, and setting up and operating testing equipment.

Surveying technicians make surveys for mapping and measuring purposes. They gather data for the design of highways and dams or for the creating of topographic maps and nautical and aeronautical charts. *Range conservationists* administer range conservation programs, which enables the livestock industry to operate their ranges more efficiently and productively.

Education and training

A high-school diploma is essential for anyone wishing to become a soil-conservation technician. High-school students should take courses in mathematics, speech, writing, chemistry, and biology. Courses in vocational agriculture, the study of farming as an occupation, are also helpful.

After high school, students should enroll in a technical institute or a junior or community college that offers an associate degree in soil

▶ On a field that was once mined for coal, a soil-conservation technician studies the health of wheat growing in the field.

conservation. First-year courses in these programs include basic soils, chemistry, botany, zoology, and introduction to range management. Second-year courses include surveying, forestry, game management, fish management, and soil and water conservation.

Earnings

Employment opportunities for soil-conservation technicians are not expected to change much during the early 1990s. Private employers will offer the best opportunities.

Technicians hired by private firms can expect starting salaries of about $12,000 to $15,000 a year. Some beginning salaries may be as high as $17,000 a year.

Ways of getting more information

For more information about a career as a soil-conservation technician, contact:

▶ American Society of Agronomy
677 South Segoe Road
Madison, WI 53711

▶ Soil Conservation Society of America
7515 NE Ankeny Road
Ankeny, IA 50021

41

Soil Scientists

Other Articles to Look At:

▶ **Agricultural Scientists**
▶ **Chemists**
▶ **Farm Operatives and Managers**
▶ **Landscape Architects**
▶ **Soil-Conservation Technicians**

What soil scientists do

Soil is one of our most important natural resources. It provides the nutrients necessary to grow food for millions of people. To use soil wisely and keep it from washing away or otherwise being damaged, experts are needed to analyze the soil and determine the best ways to manage it. *Soil scientists* are these experts. They collect soil samples and study their chemical and physical characteristics. They study how soil responds to fertilizers and other farming practices in order to help farmers decide what types of crops to grow on certain soils.

Soil scientists do much of their work outdoors. They go to fields to take soil samples, and they spend many hours meeting with farmers and discussing ways of avoiding soil damage. A soil scientist may suggest that a farmer grow crops on different parts of a farm every several years so that the unused soil can replenish itself. The soil scientist may also recommend that a farmer use various fertilizers to put nutrients back into the soil or suggest ways of covering crops to keep the wind from blowing the soil away.

Soil scientists work for agricultural research laboratories, crop production companies, and other organizations. Although they usually answer agricultural questions, these scientists also work with road departments to advise them about the quality and condition of the soil over which roads will be built.

Some soil scientists travel to foreign countries to conduct research and observe the way other scientists treat the soil. Many soil scientists are involved with teaching at colleges, universities, and agricultural schools.

Education and training

Soil scientists should have a solid background in mathematics and science, particularly the physical and earth sciences. They should also be curious, be able to solve complex problems, and have good communication skills.

The best way to become a soil scientist is to get a master's degree in agricultural science. A master's degree in biology, physics, or chemistry might also be sufficient, but some coursework in agriculture is highly desirable. A bachelor's degree in agriculture science may be adequate for some nonresearch jobs, but advancement opportunities will be limited. Many research and teaching positions require a doctorate.

High-school students should take four years of mathematics and courses in earth science, physics, and chemistry. Classes in English and history are also recommended.

▶ A soil scientist tests the ground for water levels to see if there is enough water present for the plants.

Earnings

With agricultural concerns continuing to be an important issue in the coming years, soil scientists should have good job opportunities. Many of the openings will be with private companies; the government may not be hiring many new scientists.

The average salary for those with a master's degree is about $33,000 per year; those with a doctorate should earn about $37,000 annually. Those with a bachelor's degree should earn about $24,000 per year, but job opportunities will be limited.

Ways of getting more information

In addition, write to the following organizations:

▶ Soil Conservation Society of America
  7515 NE Ankeny Road
  Ankeny, IA 50021

▶ Soil Science Society of America
  677 South Segoe Road
  Madison, WI 53711

Sound-Recording Technicians

Other Articles to Look At:

▶ **Audio-Control Technicians**
▶ **Field Technicians**
▶ **Sound-Effects Technicians**
▶ **Studio Technicians**
▶ **Transmitter Technicians**
▶ **Video Technicians**

What sound-recording technicians do

Sound-recording technicians are at the heart of any broadcast operation. These technicians, also known as *recording engineers*, operate disc and tape recording equipment. They record radio broadcast and the sound porting of television programs. They are responsible for the quality of the sound that listeners hear.

Some sound-recording technicians work in recording studios. They record the sound for musical, spoken, and dramatic phonograph records, tapes, and compact discs. They may also operate equipment that transfers sound from one medium to another—from tape to disc or from phonograph records to tape.

Sound-recording technicians load tapes into recorders, adjust volume, tone, and speed controls; and switch on correct microphone connections. During a recording, they watch meters that indicate sound levels and sound quality and adjust volume and tone controls accordingly. After recording sessions, technicians label and file tapes for quick reference.

Usually, sound-recording technicians work in studios. Sometimes, however, they may be required to work in remote locations. For example, a symphony orchestra might choose to make a recording in a church because of its special organ. This means that the sound-recording technicians must transport their portable equipment to the church and set it up there. First, the technicians decide where to place the microphones for the best sound pickup. Then they usually monitor the recording from a sound truck outside. This truck often contains much of the same equipment that is found in a studio, including tape machines and sound quality meters.

Education and training

As with all broadcast technician occupations, interested person should first graduate from high school. After high school, students should enroll in an approved community or technical college.

In high school, students should concentrate on mathematics and science courses. Students should also take any electronics courses offered, as well as courses in audio and video technology.

Sound-recording technicians who work in radio and television must be licensed if their work involves operating transmitters.

Earnings

In the early 1990s, students interested in this career will find employment opportunities to be about average. Technicians will be needed to replace those workers who leave the field or who retire.

In general, broadcast technicians can expect a starting salary of about $15,000 a year for radio work and $16,000 a year for television work. The average salary for radio broadcast technicians is $17,000 a year. The average for television broadcast technicians is $20,000 a year. Experienced senior broadcast technicians may earn $50,000 a year or more.

Ways of getting more information

For more information about a career as a sound-recording technician, contact:

▶ Broadcast Education Association
    1771 N Street, NW
    Washington, DC 20036

▶ Federal Communications Commission
    1919 M Street, NW
    Washington, DC 20554

▶ National Association of Broadcast Employees and Technicians
    7101 Wisconsin Avenue, Suite 800
    Bethesda, MD 20814

▶ At the location of the recording session, a sound-recording technician monitors the quality of the sound with his headphones.

Sound Technicians

Other Articles to Look At:

▶ **Audio-Control Technicians**
▶ **Audiovisual Technicians**
▶ **Cable-Television Technicians**
▶ **Electricians**
▶ **Recording Industry Workers**
▶ **Sound-Recording Technicians**
▶ **Telephone Installers and Repairers**

What sound technicians do

Sound technicians install, maintain, and repair sound systems that are used in businesses, offices, stores, and factories. These sound systems may be designed to play music, announce messages, or to provide the sound portion of live or recorded lectures or entertainment.

Sound technicians usually work under the direction of a sound technician supervisor who has received instructions about what kinds of equipment and connections are required for a job. After receiving instructions from the supervisor, sound technicians put the sound equipment into position and secure it in place with brackets, clamps, or screws. They install and attach the wires and cables that connect the various parts of the system, such as speakers, amplifiers, microphones, and tape players. They also test the various parts of the system to see that they are functioning properly.

Not all sound systems work the same way. For example, the sound system in a dentist's office will play mostly soothing music at a low volume. The sound system in an airport or factory, on the other hand, is used to broadcast announcements and must be loud enough to be heard over the noise of engines, machines, and people's conversations. Sound technicians help their supervisors test the systems they install to be sure they work properly for their purpose and setting. They turn volume and control knobs to adjust sound levels to suit the size of the room, the level of other noises, and the uses to which the system is being put.

After the installation, sound technicians also repair and maintain the sound equipment as necessary.

Education and training

Sound technicians need to have at least a high-school education. In addition, many employers prefer to hire applicants who have completed one or two years of post–high-school training at a trade or vocational school or at a junior or community college.

While in high school, students interested in this kind of work should take courses in mathematics and science, especially courses that include instruction in electricity, electronics, and how sound travels. The mathematics courses should include algebra and geometry. Students should also take courses in English. They should be able to read safety rules, equipment and technical manuals, and other

▶ Sound systems are installed in most public shopping areas to add pleasant atmosphere.

kinds of written instructions. They should be able to write reports with proper spelling, grammar, and punctuation.

Earnings

Sound systems will probably continue to be used in a wide variety of settings, and employment opportunities for sound technicians will probably remain quite good in the early 1990s.

The salaries of sound technicians vary according to the part of the country they work in and their level of education, experience, and responsibility. Most sound technicians are paid between $18,000 and $30,000 a year. A few, especially those with little experience or training, may make only around $14,000 a year, while some very experienced technicians may make as much as $36,000 a year or more.

Ways of getting more information

Working as an audiovisual aide or as a member of a stage crew will offer relevant experience.

In addition, students can write for more information from any of the following organizations:

▶ Electronic Industries Association
    1722 I Street, NW
    Washington, DC 20006

▶ International Society of Certified
    Electronics Technicians
    2708 West Berry
    Fort Worth, TX 76109

▶ National Electronic Service Dealers
    Association
    2708 West Berry Street
    Ft. Worth, TX 76109

Speech-Language Pathologists

Other Articles to Look At:

▶ **Audiologists**
▶ **Physical Therapists**
▶ **Psychologists**
▶ **Social Workers**

What speech-language pathologists do

Speech-language pathologists, or *therapists,* use prescribed tests to identify speech disorders in people and help them overcome their difficulties. The many speech disorders include difficulty making certain sounds, stuttering, or speaking quickly. Some people lose their ability to speak, either temporarily or totally. Most therapists work in schools, where they test students regularly for speech disorders. The students who have problems receive therapy at the school, or go to a speech clinic for treatment. There they receive physical therapy and help from psychologists and social workers. In some cases patients learn to develop entirely new speech skills, using tongue exercises and speech drills.

Speech therapy can be given individually or in groups. Usually, patients feel more comfortable when they work alone with a therapist. However, some people make more progress when they are placed with people who have similar speech problems. They seem to be encouraged by listening to the progress of others.

Not all speech therapists work in schools or privately owned speech clinics. Some work in hospitals, rehabilitation centers, and university speech clinics. Others conduct research into the causes and cures of speech disorders or teach in colleges and universities.

Education and training

Training to become a speech pathologist begins in college. Most states require a master's degree in speech pathology before entering the career. More than 200 universities and colleges offer coursework at this level.

Undergraduate courses usually include the study of the body (anatomy), child psychology, biology, physiology, and the study of speech and languages (linguistics, semantics, and phonetics).

High-school teachers in public school must earn a teacher's certificate and pass the state requirements for working with handicapped children. Those who intend on practicing speech pathology outside of a school setting, might need an additional 300 hours work experience and also have to pass an examination.

Earnings

Opportunities for employment in the early 1990s are excellent in hospitals, nursing

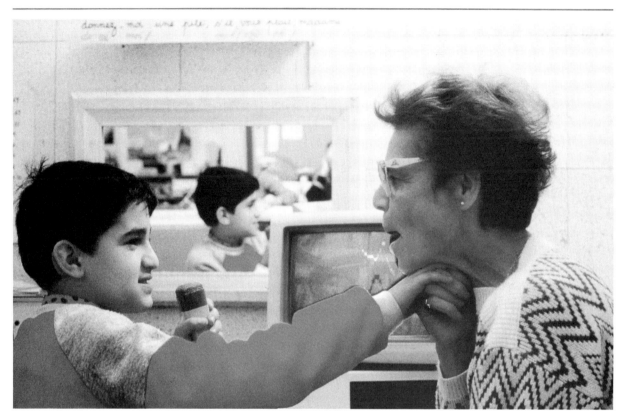

▶ Pressing the student's hand to the therapist's throat, a speech therapist shows the student how the throat should move while speaking.

homes, rehabilitation centers, and home health agencies, where recovering stroke victims need therapy. Little growth is expected in schools.

Speech pathologists' average yearly salary ranges from $23,000 to $34,000. The amount depends, however, on the individual's qualifications and experience.

Ways of getting more information

For more information about a career as a speech pathologist, contact hospitals, rehabilitation centers, and therapy clinics. Ask to interview a speech therapist about his or her work. Volunteering to work in a clinic or hospital where you can become acquainted with speech defects and their cures is a possibility as is summer and part-time work in hospitals or clinics.

For more information about a career as a speech-language pathologist write to the following sources:

▶ American Speech-Language-Hearing Association
10801 Rockville Pike
Rockville, MD 20852

Sporting Goods Production Workers

Other Articles to Look At:
- ► **Assemblers**
- ► **Heat Treaters**
- ► **Molders**
- ► **Plastics Products Manufacturing Workers**
- ► **Quality-Control Technicians**
- ► **Toy Industry Workers**

What sporting goods production workers do

Team sports and personal physical fitness have come to enjoy widespread popularity in the 1980s. Professional and college sports teams dominate radio and television and the sports pages of newspapers. Health and racquet-sports clubs have become common sources of recreation for many Americans.

This sports and fitness boom has increased the demand for a wide variety of sports equipment ranging from tennis and bowling balls to hockey and lacrosse sticks. Workers are also in demand to produce sports equipment. *Sporting goods production workers* operate the automated machinery that turns out sports equipment. In addition, many of these workers also hand-make equipment that cannot easily be produced by machines.

Many sports goods production workers are *machine operators.* The machines they operate range from sewing machines to large, complex automated equipment. These machines head, mold, stretch, cut, pound, and trim materials.

Assemblers are workers who put together the parts of products. These workers clean, paint, polish, stitch, weave, lace, glue, weld, or engrave objects. *Floor assemblers* work with power tools and large, automated machines. *Bench assemblers* do more exacting work, putting together small parts and testing finished products. *Precision assemblers* perform tasks that require special skills. These workers sometimes test new designs and products.

Many sporting goods productions workers are highly specialized. These workers include *hand baseball sewers, gold club assemblers, base fillers and stuffers, baseball glove shapers, inflated ball molders,* and *bowling balling engravers.*

The quality of sporting goods is important, especially for equipment that is to be used in college and professional sports. Many team sports have strict rules and regulations regarding the size and shape of equipment as well as the materials used in manufacturing it. *Quality control inspectors* make sure that all manufactured equipment conforms to these rules and regulations.

Education and training

For most manufacturing work, a high-school diploma is desires, although it is not always necessary. New employees must often receive on-the-job training. Depending on the type of manufacturing operation involved, this training may last from just a few days up to several months.

Earnings

Even though Americans are spending more of their time and money on recreation, much of the sports equipment is imported causing a reduction in manufacturing workers. There will be little change in the need for workers in this field during the early 1990s.

Most sporting goods productions workers receive at least the minimum wage as a starting salary. Beginning pay ranges from $10,000 to $18,000 per year. Assemblers usually earn from $9,300 to $19,000 per year. Skilled machine operators earn a higher wage. Average pay for all sporting goods production workers is about $7.00 an hour.

Ways of getting more information

For more information about a career as a sporting goods production worker, contact:

▶ Sporting Goods Publishing Company
1212 North Lindbergh Boulevard
St. Louis, MO 63132

▶ A sporting goods production worker prepares footballs for the installment of the inflatable bladders.

Sports Coaches

Other Articles to Look At:

▶ **Athletics**
▶ **Athletic Trainers**
▶ **Recreation Workers**
▶ **Sports Instructors**

What sports coaches do

Organized sports teams at every age level and level of competition. For example, children as young as six and seven years of age can join baseball and soccer leagues. These same children can progress through pony leagues, little league sports, grammar school teams, and high-school and college teams. As adults, some may even become members of professional sports teams or play on neighborhood or work-related teams.

All of these teams in all sports have one common element—a coach. Sports coaches, sometimes called *athletic coaches,* fall into two general categories: *head coaches* and *professional athletes coaches.* Head coaches lead teams of athletes. Professional athlete coaches often work with athletes in individual sports, such as tennis and golf. In either case, the primary role of the coach is to teach and inspire players and to produce winners.

Coaches must be very knowledgeable about the rules and strategies of their sport. They must be able to analyze the performance of their players and to fit players into positions where they can contribute the most to their teams. This analysis often involves reviewing videotapes of players' performances.

Coaches often work with *assistant coaches* who usually concentrate on one specific aspect of the sport. For example, baseball teams usually employ pitching coaches, hitting coaches, outfield coaches, and first- and third-base coaches. Football teams have offensive coaches, defensive coaches, linebacker coaches, and quarterback coaches. All of these assistant coaches work under the direction of the head coach.

Education and training

There are no specific educational requirements for coaches. Many of today's coaches have college degrees because they played college sports. Nevertheless, it is possible for anyone with knowledge and love of a sport and excellent leadership qualities to become a coach.

Coaches usually work their way up through the coaching system. Most begin as assistant coaches on little league or grammar school teams. These coaches may eventually become head coaches on high-school or college teams. The very best of these coaches often go on to coach world-class athletes or professional sports teams.

Earnings

Americans are avid sports fans and enjoy both watching and playing team sports. Both young and old alike will participate in more sports during the early 1990s, requiring more coaches to lead the players.

In the sports of professional football, basketball, and baseball, head coaches usually earn between $50,000 and $250,000 a year. A professional coach's salary is often directly related do how successful the coach has been in producing winning teams.

College coaches earn an average salary of about $35,000, although coaches at big universities often earn much more. High-school coaches generally earn between $15,000 and $30,000 per year. In addition to coaching, high-school coaches often teach classes as well.

Ways of getting more information

To obtain more information about a career as a sports coach, write to the following:

▶ American Alliance for Health, Physical Education, Recreation and Dance
    1900 Association Drive
    Reston, VA 22091

▶ The Athletic Institute
    200 Castlewood Drive
    North Palm Beach, FL 33408

▶ Society of State Directors of Health, Physical Education, and Recreation
    9805 Hillridge Drive
    Kensington, MD 20895

▶ A coach explains a plan of defense for the game to his basketball team.

Stage Production Workers

Other Articles to Look At:

▶ **Actors and Actresses**
▶ **Designers**
▶ **Light Technicians**
▶ **Sound Technicians**
▶ **Stage Technicians**

What stage production workers do

Stage production workers work behind the scenes of a play or other theatrical performance, handling a variety of tasks to add to the impact of the performance and keep it running smoothly. Because they are involved with all aspects of the performance, their specific responsibilities vary according to their job title. Stage production work is necessary for plays, operas, ballets, and other performances in theaters. These workers can also find work in concerts, lectures, and award ceremonies and dinners.

Concert or *lecture hall managers* supervise the theater itself. They manage the ticket takers and ushers, maintain the physical building, order food for the refreshment counter and other supplies, and are on hand during performances to answer questions and handle problems. *Road production general managers* perform basically the same tasks when a play travels to other cities, or goes "on tour." They also arrange for housing for the crew and cast, handle advertising and promotion, and oversee the hiring of any stagehands while on tour.

Stage directors are in charge of the actual production of the play itself. They hire the cast and supervise rehearsals, and go on to work with playwrights, producers, set and costume designers, lighting and sound technicians, and stage managers to make sure the play is presented as effectively as possible.

There are all kinds of other backstage workers. *Set designers* design and supervise the construction of the scenery, and *costume designers* design and supervise the buying or making of the costumes; each of them has assistants and crews working under them. *Prop managers* are in charge of finding, buying, or making all the things the actors and actresses use on stage. The technical designers and workers are the people who plan and operate the lighting and sound effects needed to make the play truly dramatic. Finally there is the *stage manager,* who acts as a sort of director's assistant to coordinate all the various parts of backstage work.

Education and training

Although there are no specific educational requirements for stage production workers, a high-school diploma is usually required, and a college degree is highly recommended. Drama courses and experience in school theatrical performances are obvious pluses, and specific skills such as design or fine arts for set and costume designers; business courses for concert hall and road production managers are also helpful. Courses in drawing, painting, sewing, wood work shop, architectural drawing, and shop are all helpful preparations for a career in stage production.

Most stage production workers begin by volunteering their services or by working part-time in a position not directly related to the one they really want. Set designers might start as members of the set construction crew; a director might begin as an assistant stage manager. Gradually the skilled worker may work his or her way up to the desired position; it should be noted that the competition for theatrical work is very keen, and even experienced workers often work part-time or in assistant positions.

Earnings

Salaries for stage productions workers vary enormously, depending on the experience of the worker, specific job responsibilities, location of the theater, and budget of the performance. Successful Broadway directors may earn well more than $200,000 a year; struggling regional or off-Broadway directors may have to supplement their income by waiting tables. Some jobs are governed by union rates, which means the hourly, daily, or weekly rate may be quite good; keep in mind that few stage production workers work year-round. Many of them only work part-time and must have other jobs.

Ways of getting more information

Getting involved with school or community theatrical performances is the best way to test interests and talents in this field.

For more information about stage production work, write to:

▶ A stage production worker hems a costume for a cast member.

▶ International Alliance of Theatrical Stage Employees and Moving Picture Machine Operators of the United States and Canada
   1515 Broadway
   New York, NY 10036

▶ Society of Stage Directors and Choreographers
   1501 Broadway
   New York, NY 10036

▶ United Scenic Artists
   575 8th Avenue
   New York, NY 10018

Stage Technicians

Other Articles to Look At:

▶ **Audiovisual Technicians**
▶ **Carpenters**
▶ **Electricians**
▶ **Light Technicians**
▶ **Stage Production Workers**

What stage technicians do

Stage technicians install lights, sound equipment, and scenery for theater stages. They also build stages for theatrical and musical events in parks, stadiums, and other places.

In carrying out a project, stage technicians use diagrams of the stage and written instructions from the stage designer. They confer with the stage manager to decide what kinds of sets, scenery, props, lighting, and sound equipment are required.

Then they collect or build the props or scenery, using hammers, saws, and other handtools and power tools. Often they must climb ladders, scaffolding, or beams near the ceiling to connect cables or ropes that are used to raise and lower curtains or scenery.

Stage technicians also position lights and sound equipment on or around the stage. They clamp light fixtures to supports and connect electrical wiring from the fixtures to power sources and control panels.

The sound equipment used on and around stages usually includes microphones, speakers, and amplifiers. Technicians position this equipment and attach the wires that connect it to power sources and to the sound-mixing equipment that controls the volume and quality of the sound.

During rehearsals and performances, stage technicians may pull ropes and cables that raise and lower curtains and other equipment. Sometimes they also operate the lighting and sound equipment.

Education and training

Stage technicians usually must be high-school graduates. In addition, many employers prefer to hire stage technicians who are graduates of two-year junior or community colleges. While in high school, people interested in this career should take college-preparatory courses, including algebra and geometry and English courses that develop their reading and writing skills.

During their post–high-school training, students should take any available courses in theater arts or related subjects, along with general-studies courses, especially in English and music. They should also take carpentry or electronics, especially those that include work with lighting and sound.

Earnings

It is almost impossible to foresee what employment opportunities for stage technicians will be like in the future. The demand for stage technicians is determined by the amount of live entertainment that is being of-

▶ A stage technician checks the positions of spotlights during a technical rehearsal.

fered, and that is strongly influenced by over-all economic conditions. If the economy remains strong, employment opportunities should be good.

Most stage technicians earn between $20,000 and $30,000 a year; however, salaries vary widely depending on the employer, geographical location, and the technician's level of responsibility. Beginning technicians may earn less than $20,000 a year.

Stage technicians who are hired mostly for their skills as carpenters, electricians, or sound or light technicians earn salaries roughly equal to the salaries received by those workers. The salaries for most workers in these careers range from $14,000 to $30,000 a year, with carpenters generally at the low end and electricians at the high end.

Ways of getting more information

Probably the best way to learn more about this kind of work is through personal experience as a stage hand helping to put on a school show or play. Another way of getting more information is to ask a teacher or guidance counselor to arrange a visit to a local theater where students can meet and talk to stage technicians. A summer job in a theater is another good way to get experience.

In addition, students can write for more information from the following organization:

▶ Theater Communications Group
355 Lexington Avenue
New York, NY 10017

State Police Officers

Other Articles to Look At:

▶ **Crime Laboratory Technicians**
▶ **FBI Agents**
▶ **Fire Fighters**
▶ **Lawyers and Judges**
▶ **Police Officers**

What state police officers do

State police officers patrol our highways and enforce highway safety laws. The state police is a fairly new agency, started within the last 100 years. Highway use is one example of why the state police came into being: If a car is going twenty miles an hour over the speed limit and a police officer from a local force chases the driver on an interstate, the two cars could easily leave the borders of one town or county and go into another, where the police officer would have no jurisdiction and where he or she would therefore be unable to write a ticket or make an arrest. State police officers can enforce the law anywhere within the borders of their state.

As highway safety officers, state police ride in patrol cars looking out for dangerous situations. They write traffic tickets, give warnings, and watch for stolen vehicles. They also help drivers who are having trouble with their cars or trucks. If there is a highway accident, state police officers take charge at the scene, directing traffic, calling for emergency equipment, and giving first aid.

In additional to highway safety, state police officers do some general police work such as keeping order and catching criminals. *Detectives* and *investigators* work in plainclothes and try to gather information about criminals. They look over the scene of a crime, collect evidence, question witnesses, and write reports. After a criminal has been caught, detectives appear in court and give the evidence they have collected.

Education and training

Each state has its own special requirements for their officers but some apply to all states. Candidates must be United States citizens and pass a tough examination. They must also have a high-school diploma, be at least twenty-one, and have a valid driver's license. The best-prepared candidates will have taken some college courses in subjects such as English, government, and the sciences. Police training with one of the armed forces is also very helpful. Candidates also have to pass difficult physical tests because officers must have better than average strength and stamina.

Once candidates are accepted into a training program, they take classes in such areas as their state's laws, self-defense, first-aid, and how to handle firearms.

Experienced officers are usually able to advance by taking college classes in police science and law enforcement. Officers move up on the basis of job performance, outside training, and good conduct. The usual way to move up the ranks is from private, to corporal, to sergeant, to first sergeant, to lieutenant, and finally to captain.

Earnings

It is expected that state patrols will need more officers in the early 1990s. Competition for these jobs will be heavy as more and more men, women, and minorities try to enter this field.

In the early 1990s new officers earned $18,000 per year, with the average for all officers was about $20,000. Salaries increase with experience though—sergeants earn $23,000, lieutenants about $30,000, and captains $40,000 or more.

Ways of getting more information

The best way to prepare for the job is to take classes in English and government and to learn to be a good driver through driver's education classes.

Write to the following for more information on state police officers:

▶ American Police Academy
Lock Box 15350
Chevy Chase, MD 20815

▷ A state police officer lectures a class on drug related problems.

Statistical Clerks

Other Articles to Look At:

▶ **Accountants**
▶ **Billing clerks**
▶ **Bookkeepers**
▶ **File Clerks**
▶ **Insurance Claims Representatives**

What statistical clerks do

Statistical clerks help collect and organize the information that business and government leaders need to make accurate decisions. They collect sales records, survey results, and other types of numerical data and organize it so that it can be used for further study. They add and subtract numbers, put specific information into certain categories, and organize the information in other ways. They often present information such as the number of products sold in one month or how many hours people worked over a period of time by using graphs and charts so that it can be understood more quickly and accurately.

Statistical clerks work for all types of businesses and other organizations, and their responsibilities are somewhat different depending on who they work for. For example, a clerk who works for a hospital might collect statistics on the number of patients in the hospital over a one month period and how much it cost the hospital to treat each patient. This information might be used to help decide whether to buy equipment that would help the hospital treat patients more efficiently. Clerks for an insurance company might be asked to collect information on how many accidents various types of clients have had and this information might to used to develop new insurance rates.

Clerks often collect the needed information from several different sources. They may check sales records, questionnaire results, and production records to get information. Clerks either record information by writing it in a business notebook or by entering the data into a computer terminal. Clerks must carefully check the information as they enter it so that they only use accurate information. They also double check their work to make sure any mathematical work was done correctly. Clerks perform many of the organizational tasks by hand; however they generally use computers, adding machines, or other office machines to do the mathematical work.

Statistical clerks often work alongside bookkeepers and accountants to perform calculations and prepare statistical reports. Often, an accountant will supervise the clerk as the clerk checks sales information and other statistics.

Education and training

Statistical clerks should be able to operate computers, adding machines, and other types of office machinery and have good mathematical skills. Clerks must be able to do the same tasks over and over again while maintaining their concentration. They must also have clear handwriting.

Most statistical clerks are high-school graduates with good mathematical skills. Those with typing and bookkeeping skills and some experience working in an office setting have the best chances at finding employment. Employers usually provide on-the-job training during which time new clerks work under the supervision of more experienced clerks. They learn how to collect and organize the statistical information and operate the computers and other office equipment.

Many community colleges and vocational schools offer business education courses that provide additional training for clerks in the areas of bookkeeping, typing, computer operations, and office procedures.

▶ Comparing the original data against the graphs, a statistical clerk prepares information in graph form.

Earnings

Although the amount of statistical information needed to be processed is expected to increase, job openings for clerks will decrease during the early 1990s. This is because computers and other types of automated office equipment can now do many of the record-keeping tasks previously done by clerks. Job opportunities will be best for those who know how to operate computers and have had some previous office experience.

The average beginning salary is about $18,000 per year, with experienced clerks earning about $22,000 annually. Those people with computer skills will earn the highest salaries.

Ways of getting more information

It may be possible to get a part-time or summer job in an office and in that way learn more about the profession.

In addition, write to the following organization:

▶ American Statistical Association
1429 Duke Street
Alexandria, VA 22314

Stenographers

Other Articles to Look At:

▶ **Bookkeepers**
▶ **Court Reporters**
▶ **Medical Record Administrators**
▶ **Receptionists**
▶ **Secretaries**

What stenographers do

Stenographers write down what people say as they say it. This is called "taking dictation." Because they have to work very quickly, stenographers use shorthand, a set of symbols that stand for words and parts of words. They may write shorthand or use a stenotype machine that types shorthand symbols. Then they transcribe their shorthand notes and type them up into letters, reports, or other documents. Stenographers are also called *stenotype operators.*

Using a stenographer saves time; instead of writing out letters and memos, the stenographers' employers can simply tell the stenographer what they want to say. The stenographer returns a finished document.

General stenographers take routine dictation and do other office tasks such as typing, filing, and answering telephones. Experienced stenographers take more difficult dictations; for example, they may sit in on staff meeting and later give word-for-word records or summary reports of the meeting. Experienced stenographers may also supervise other stenographers and office clerical workers.

Some stenographers develop special skills. Technical stenographers master the terms of a specialized field such as law, medicine, or engineering. Some stenographer can take dictation in foreign languages.

Other stenographers, called *shorthand reporters* are responsible for making the official records of government meetings. Shorthand reporters may record a meeting of the U.S. Congress or a state legislature or other government agency. Accuracy is extremely important. Many shorthand reporters use a computer system, called Computer-Aided Transcription, which can translate shorthand notes into English.

Education and training

Stenographers need a high-school diploma. High-school courses in typing, shorthand, and business English are good preparation. Business schools and vocational schools also teach stenographic skills. Getting jobs and advancement will depend on a stenographer's speed and accuracy at both taking dictation and typing. The federal government requires stenographers to take dictation at eighty words a minute and type forty words a minute. Many shorthand reporters must be able to take dictation at 225 words a minute.

Earnings

There will be a declining number of job openings for stenographers in the 1990s because

▶ A stenographer takes dictation from her employer, using a shorthand method of writing that saves time.

many offices now use dictation machines. However, the federal government as well as state and local governments and conferences will continue to need skilled shorthand reporters.

General stenographers working in private industry earn about $18,400. Experienced stenographers average $21,700. The federal government pays between $10,815 and $14,822 a year.

Ways of getting more information

Acting as a club or organization's secretary would be a good introduction to the work for a stenographer. High-school business and secretarial courses are also valuable.

For more information write to:

▶ Association of Independent Colleges and Schools
   1 Dupont Circle, NW, Suite 350
   Washington, DC 20036

▶ National Shorthand Reporters Association
   118 Park Street, SE
   Vienna, VA 22180

Stevedores

Other Articles to Look At:

▶ **Industrial Truck Operators**
▶ **Manufacturing Truck Supervisors**
▶ **Merchant Marine Workers**
▶ **Military Careers**
▶ **Operating Engineers**
▶ **Shipping and Receiving Clerks**
▶ **Traffic Agents and Clerks**

What stevedores do

When a ship comes into a busy port, *stevedores* are there ready to unload the cargo and deliver it to trucks. When the ship's cargo hold is empty, stevedores reload it and make sure all is in order before the ship leaves the pier and heads for another port.

Stevedores, also called *longshore workers,* first dock ships by tying lines. Their work then breaks down into several categories: *Dock workers* handle cargo on the pier, while *hold workers* go into the ship's hold, remove cargo from hooks, and stow it in place. *Winch operators* handle the winches that control the booms that raise or lower cargo from the ship's deck. *Drivers* operate the fork lift trucks, cranes, and other equipment. *Gear workers* maintain and repair the nets that prevent cargo that is accidentally dropped from the boom from falling into the water. The title *stevedores,* besides referring to the field in general, is also the name of one job in particular. The stevedore is in charge of stowing

the cargo on a vessel as well as for all the workers on board. On large ships there can be as many as 250 longshore workers loading and unloading cargo.

Finally, *pier superintendents* are in charge of the operations of the entire pier. They study the layout of the ship so they know where the cargo should go—for example, cargo that is to be delivered at the next port must be loaded last. They know how many workers they need for the number of ships arriving, and they then hire those workers. They figure out how much the operation of their pier costs, and they make sure the bills are both sent out and collected.

Education and training

Stevedores must be physically strong and have plenty of stamina. Their work demands much of their bodies and can sometimes be dangerous. Because of this workers must be constantly alert and able to follow instructions.

Those who are in supervisor's jobs must have a good understanding of the entire operation of loading and unloading a ship. These workers often receive their training from one of the several U.S. maritime academies.

Earnings

In the early 1990s, there is a demand for stevedores in some areas of the country. The Great Lakes area, for example, is in need of trained workers. It has only been fairly recently that ocean-going ships could sail these inland lakes, and so the stevedoring industry there is not well developed. In other areas, automated loaders have taken the places of some stevedores, but there is still a need for full-time trained longshore workers.

Longshore workers on the East Coast earned a base salary of $25,000 in the early 1990s. Pier superintendents made between $20,000 and $35,000 per year, depending on the area of the country.

Ways of getting more information

For more information about stevedoring careers write to the following:

▶ The International Longshoremen's and Warehousemen's Union
1188 Franklin Street
San Francisco, CA 94109

▶ International Longshoremen's Association
17 Battery Park, Room 1530
New York, NY 10004

▶ Stevedores guide lift operators to move cables into place to unload freight from a ship.

Stockbrokers

Other Articles to Look At:

▶ **Bank Tellers**
▶ **Bank Officers and Managers**
▶ **Life Insurance Agents and Brokers**
▶ **Real Estate Agents and Brokers**
▶ **Services Sales Representatives**

What stockbrokers do

Stockbrokers represent both individuals and organizations in the buying and selling of stocks. When people buy stock, or shares, in a company, they actually own part of the company. Company managers use the money from the sale of stock to try to make the company more profitable. When the price of a stock goes up, stock owners may decide to sell their shares to make a profit. If they sell when the price has gone down, they have to take a loss. The price at any given time depends on the demand for the stock.

Stockbrokers may also be called *securities sales workers* or *account executives*. They perform a variety of duties. They open accounts for new customers. In doing so, they have to gather certain information from customers. This information is required before customers can buy and sell stocks through a stockbroker's company. To do so, they send the information to the floor of a stock exchange. A stock exchange is a place where stocks are bought and sold.

Stockbrokers give information to customers about the future outlook of companies. They may give advice to customers about when to buy or sell certain stocks. They must be prepared to answer any question customers may have about how the stock market operates. They have to keep accurate records of all stock sales and purchases made on behalf of customers. In addition, they have to find new customers.

Stockbrokers are employed by companies know as brokerage houses which are located throughout the country. During busy times, they may have to work overtime to keep up with paperwork. They may work fewer hours when they have few customers orders to carry out.

Education and training

Most brokerage houses will hire only people with college degrees. Some prefer those with degrees in business management and finance. Employees are given on-the-job training at most brokerage houses.

Almost all states require stockbrokers to be licensed. They are sometimes given written tests. In some cases they have to post a personal bond. Stockbrokers also have to register as representatives of their company. In doing so, they must obey the rules of the stock exchange they deal with, or the rules of the National Association of Security Dealers. To become a registered representative, stockbrokers must also pass a test.

▶ A stock broker calls up the current prices for a stock on his computer terminal.

Earnings

The job outlook for stockbrokers is good through the early 1990s. The economy is growing. Thus, more companies will need to raise money through the sale of stock. Also, individuals have more money to invest in the stock market. Demand for stockbrokers goes up and down with the economy. Many beginning brokers are unable to find and keep enough customers, so they leave the field. This creates more job openings. There is much competition in this field.

The salaries of beginners averaged about $37,000 per year. Larger companies pay a somewhat higher starting wage. Once stockbrokers have enough customers, they work only on a commission basis. Experienced stockbrokers dealing with individual investors made an average of about $91,000 per year in the early 1990s. Those who helped institutions invest money earned an average of about $227,000 per year. Brokerage houses may pay annual bonuses to brokers.

Ways of getting more information

Visiting a brokerage or a stock exchange in or near your community is an excellent introduction to this career.

For more information write to:

▶ American Stock Exchange
   86 Trinity Place
   New York, NY 10006

▶ New York Stock Exchange
   11 Wall Street
   New York, NY 10005

▶ Securities Industries Association
   120 Broadway
   New York, NY 10271

Stock Clerks

Other Articles to Look At:

▶ **Cashiers**
▶ **General Office Clerks**
▶ **Hotel Clerks**
▶ **Purchasing Agents**
▶ **Shipping and Receiving Clerks**

What stock clerks do

"Stock" can best be described as the equipment, supplies, and other materials that are used or sold by businesses, industries, and institutions. *Stock clerks* receive, sort, store, and give out these materials. They work in stockroom and warehouses.

A stock clerk's job can be divided into separate tasks. First, stock clerks receive incoming goods. The clerks check the goods against invoices to make sure that everything that was supposed to be delivered is present. Then they check the goods themselves to make sure nothing has been damaged in shipping. If damage has occurred, the clerks make arrangements for the goods to be returned. Finally, the clerks keep records of what has been delivered, sent back, and so on. Today, these records are most often kept on a computer data base.

After the stock has been checked in, the clerks store it. They may put items on shelves, in bins, or on specially set off sections of the floor. If the stock is heavy, the clerks may move it around with hand trucks or with electric trucks. As the stock is put away, the clerks often code it with special numbers or with computer bar codes.

Requests for stock come in on a daily basis. In a department store, for example, the manager of the book department may submit a request for copies of twenty or thirty different books to restock the shelves. The stock clerks read the request and begin retrieving the books from wherever they have been stored. First, the clerks check an inventory record. This tells them how much of each item, in this case books, is in stock. If all of the books that the book department manager requested are in stock, the clerks load them onto carts or hand trucks. Then the clerks adjust the inventory records to show that the books have been taken out of stock. Finally, the clerks deliver the books to the manager.

In some businesses, stock clerks are also responsible for ordering stock. When supplies dip below a certain level, the clerks fill out orders for new stock. In larger businesses, this task is often handled by purchasing agents.

Education and training

There are no formal educational requirements for stock clerks. People with little education can often get jobs as receiving clerks and delivery persons. The ability to read is essential. A high-school diploma is usually required for advancement beyond these entry-level positions.

Stock clerks who want to work in large

computerized warehouses may need computer training before they can be hired. Computer skills are often taught in high school or at technical schools. Any other required training is usually given on the job.

Earnings

Automation through the use of computers will hold steady employment opportunities through the early 1990s. However, this occupation is very large and openings will occur as workers transfer to other jobs or retire.

Stock clerks usually start at the minimum wage. The average pay for experienced clerks is about $9,000 to $12,000 per year. Clerks earn time-and-a-half pay whenever they work overtime. Supervisors earn the highest pay.

Ways of getting more information

For part-time and summer jobs are often available to students. This would be a fine introduction to the work of stock clerks.

For more information about a career as a stock clerk, contact:

▶ Food Marketing Institute
1750 K Street, NW
Washington, DC 20006

▶ National Learning Corporation
212 Michael Drive
Syosset, NY 11791

▶ A stock clerk pulls pants from the back storage room when the stock is low in the store.

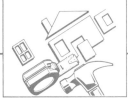

Structural-Steel Workers

Other Articles to Look At:

▶ **Cement Masons**
▶ **Construction Workers**
▶ **Forge Shop Workers**
▶ **Iron and Steel Industry Workers**
▶ **Operating Engineers**
▶ **Welders**

What structural-steel workers do
Structural-steel workers put up and put together the metal beams, columns, and frames that form the "skeleton" of a building. Also called *iron workers,* they work together as a team to raise up these heavy metal parts, place them in position, and join them together. Welding, riveting, and bolting are the usual ways of joining metal, and structural-steel workers must be good at all three. Besides large buildings, these skilled workers help build bridges and metal storage tanks.

There are several specialties within the structural-steel trade. Some structural-steel workers work as riggers and machine movers. They set up the equipment that hoists steel beams to be positioned by other workers. After deciding the best way for the steel part to be moved, they attach it to the proper lifting machines. *Reinforcing metalworkers* position the steel rods or steel mesh around which concrete is poured for columns, arches, domes, walls, and floors. *Ornamental iron-workers* put together metal stairways, doors, and cabinets. They build safes for banks and install iron fences, gates, and lampposts.

Structural-steel workers usually work outdoors and in very high places. Workers must be strong and steady, have a good sense of balance, and not be afraid of heights. They may have periods of unemployment between jobs and during bad or cold weather.

Education and training
The usual way of becoming a structural-steel worker is to complete an apprenticeship program. The International Association of Bridge, Structural and Ornamental Iron Workers can provide information on getting into these programs. An apprenticeship lasts three years and combines on-the-job training and classroom instruction. Apprentices learn to do ornamental iron and steel work, steel reinforcing, structural steel work, and welding. Each year the apprentice also takes at least 144 hours of classes in welding, blueprint reading, use of tools, and other construction-industry skills.

Earnings
Although machines are replacing many human workers in the construction industry, there will continue to be a healthy demand for structural-steel workers. Construction in general is expected to increase in the early 1990s, and more smaller buildings are being built with structural steel.

The average yearly salary for structural-

▶ A structural steel worker guides support beams into place during building construction.

steel workers in the early 1990s was around $25,000. Ornamental ironworkers earned about the same annual salary as structural workers. Workers usually receive twice their hourly rate for overtime hours. The starting pay for apprentices is about 60 to 70 percent of the salary that a skilled worker receives.

Ways of getting more information
By taking a field trip to a construction site, young people can watch structural-steel workers in action and see how their work coordinates with that of other construction workers.

For more information about structural-steel workers and their jobs write to the following:

▶ Associated General Contractors of America
  1957 E Street, NW
  Washington, DC 20006

▶ International Association of Bridge, Structural and Ornamental Iron Workers
  1750 New York Avenue, NW
  Washington, DC 20006

Studio Technicians

Other Articles to Look At:

▶ **Audio-Control Technicians**
▶ **Drafters**
▶ **Electronics Test Technicians**
▶ **Recording Industry Workers**
▶ **Sound-Recording Technicians**

What studio technicians do

Studio technicians, or *sound mixers,* are concerned with the quality of audio recordings made during the production of radio and television programs and the sound recordings made during the production of records, tapes, and compact discs. They set up and monitor sound recording equipment and operate consoles (control panels with dials and switches) to regulate the sound volume as it is being recorded.

Studio technicians control a variety of factors that influence the quality of sound recordings. They set up different combinations and arrangements of microphones and amplifiers in the studio to best achieve the desired sound for the production. In addition to arranging the equipment, they turn the microphones on and off so that they are only working when needed. This keeps unwanted sounds from being recorded. Technicians also instruct actors, actresses, and other performers which microphones are on and how loud or soft their voices (or instruments) should be.

Studio technicians work closely with *audio-control technicians, sound-recording technicians,* and other members of the broadcast production team. Before a program begins, these technicians may meet and discuss the needs of a particular production. During the taping of a program, the studio technician will often communicate with other crew members through a headset. Although the studio technician works under the supervision of the director of a production, the director often relies on the expertise of the sound technician to improve the quality of a recording.

Technicians not only set up and operate the sound recording equipment, they also maintain the equipment so that it is in good working condition. They use testing equipment such as a voltage meter to make sure the electrical wires are connected and there are no other defects. Technicians will often repair or replace broken sound recording equipment.

Education and training

Studio technicians need the electronics training and hand coordination necessary to operate technical equipment. They also should have good communication skills and be able to work closely with other audio-production workers.

The best way to become a studio technician is to have a high-school degree and at least some electronics training. Many community colleges and technical schools have programs in electronics that provide the background necessary for success in this field. Knowledge of computers is also helpful, as computers are becoming more and more important in radio and TV broadcasting.

All studio technicians are given on-the-job training and spend the first several months working under the supervision of experienced technicians. New workers are closely supervised as they set up microphones and do other necessary tasks.

Earnings

With the many radio and television stations and sound recording studios in operation, there should be a good number of job opportunities for studio technicians. However, due in part to the excitement of working as part of a production crew, there will be stiff competition for these positions. Those without much experience may have more success in smaller cities, where there are not as many job seekers.

The average salary is about $22,000 per year, with those working for television stations earning somewhat more than other technicians. Those employed in large cities will earn about twice as much as those in smaller communities. This is a major reason why there is less competition for jobs in smaller communities.

Ways of getting more information

High-school radio and television courses are a good way to gain some experience actually working on a production.

In addition, write to the following organizations and ask for information about being a studio technician:

▶ The sound board and recording tapes are continually monitored by the studio technician.

▶ Broadcast Education Association
National Association of Broadcasters
1771 N Street, NW
Washington, DC 20036

▶ National Association of Broadcast Employees and Technicians
7101 Wisconsin Avenue, Suite 800
Bethesda, MD 20814

Surgeons

Other Articles to Look At:

▶ **Hospital Attendants**
▶ **Nurse Anesthetists**
▶ **Physical Therapists**
▶ **Physicians**
▶ **Surgical Technicians**

What surgeons do

Surgeons are physicians who specialize in performing operations. They operate on patients to repair injuries; to remove diseased parts of the body; and to fix deformed parts of the body.

Some surgeons called *general surgeons* perform many different kinds of operations. Other surgeons specialize in certain operations or part of the body. For example, some surgeons operate on the brain and spinal cord. Others work on fixing broken bones. Some specialize in heart bypasses and heart transplants.

Surgeons first examine their patients, learn about their medical histories, and study the results of any physical tests. They work with the patients physicians and other medical professionals to decide if a patient needs surgery. Surgeons explain the surgery to the patient; they decide what kind of operation will work the best.

During the operation, the surgeon is the head of the medical team that works on the patient. The team will include an *anesthesiol-*

ogist, who will help the patient fall asleep during the operation, surgical assistants, and nurses. Medical students may watch the operation to learn how to do it. After operations, surgeons continue to check on their patients and check on their recovery.

Surgeons use many kinds of instruments during surgery. For example, a surgeon may cut out diseased tissue with a sharp cutting tools or with lasers. During their careers, surgeons must keep studying new methods and learning how to use new technology.

Surgeons work in hospitals and clinics. They often work under pressure because operations can be a matter of life or death for their patients. They also work long hours. They may have to perform emergency operations at night, on weekends, or on their days off. Difficult operations may involve hours of standing and demand great concentration, skill, and steadiness.

Education and training

Becoming a surgeon takes up to fourteen years of study and training. In high school, students should get a well-rounded education. Biology or chemistry are good majors for students planning on becoming surgeons. While they are in college, students take the Medical College Admission Test. Medical schools use these test scores to decide which students to accept.

After graduating from college, students spend four years in medical school. Two years of medical school concentrate on classroom and laboratory work; during the last two years, students start working with patients in hospitals.

After completing medical school, surgeons spend three to six years in a hospital residency program. As residents, they can perform operations under the supervision of the hospital's surgeons.

At the end of their training, surgeons must be certified before they can practice. To earn certification, they have to pass an examination that is administered by the state in which they wish to practice.

Earnings

The need for surgeons will grow slowly into the 1990s.

Surgeons earn between $60,000 and $175,000 a year. Some specialists earn even more. However, the education and training period for physicians and especially surgeons is long. Surgeons just out of medical school can expect to earn about $24,000 to $26,000 per year. Once they are established their incomes rise rapidly.

Ways of getting more information

You may be able to interview a surgeon or a physician about performing surgery. A librarian can help you find books and articles about surgeons and surgery.

For more information, write to the following addresses:

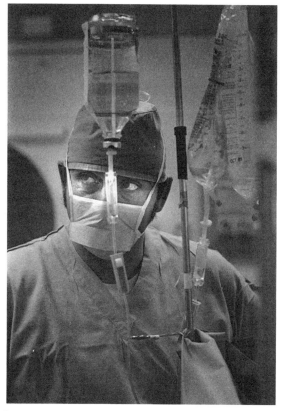

▶ A surgeon checks the patient's heart monitor during an operation.

▶ American Medical Association
535 North Dearborn Street
Chicago, IL 60610

▶ Association of American Medical Colleges
One Dupont Circle, NW
Washington, DC 20036

Surgical Technicians

Other Articles to Look At:

▶ **Biomedical Equipment Technicians**
▶ **Cardiac-Monitor Technicians**
▶ **Emergency Medical Technicians**
▶ **Hospital Attendants**
▶ **Licensed Practical Nurses**
▶ **Nurse Anesthetists**

What surgical technicians do

At one time, most surgical procedures were performed by a surgeon and an assistant. Modern operating rooms and techniques, however, require many more people working as a team. Surgical technicians are part of that team. They assist physicians, nurses, and other operating room personnel before, during, and after surgery.

The task of surgical technicians can be divided into three stages: preoperative (before surgery), intraoperative (during surgery), and postoperative (after surgery). Before surgery, technicians scrub in for surgery. This means they scrub their hands and arms before putting on their surgical gowns and gloves. Then they set out sterilized instruments and prepare other operating equipment and supplies. Technicians are also responsible for seeing that all necessary supplies are available during surgery. These supplies include linens, blood, and other solutions for use during surgery. Technicians assist other surgical personnel in putting on their gowns and gloves. Sometimes the surgical technicians are also responsible for washing, shaving, or sterilizing the surgical area.

During surgery, technicians pass instruments and supplies to the surgeon. They may hold retractors (instruments that keep incisions open) and cut stitches. They also adjust lights and may assist in administering blood and other fluids and injections. If specimens, pieces of bone or tissue, are removed during surgery, technicians care for and dispose of them. Technicians help apply dressings and operate equipment such as suctioning devices and sterilizers.

After surgery, surgical technicians help transfer the patient from the operating table to a bed in the recovery room. Then the technicians begin cleaning up the operating room. They clean and sterilize all of the instruments used during surgery and repack them into sets for use during another operation.

Education and training

Students interested in becoming surgical technicians must earn a high-school diploma. During high school, students should take courses in mathematics, science, and language.

After high school, students should enroll in a technical school or community college that offers a program for surgical technicians. Such programs usually last two years. Students will take courses in biology, microbiology, medical ethics and responsibilities,

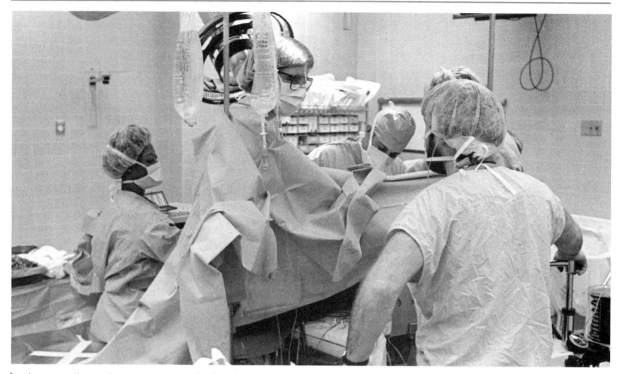

► In a sterile environment, a surgical technician prepares equipment for a patient's surgery.

anatomy, medical terminology, operating room procedures, and English.

Many hospitals require that their surgical technicians be certified by the Association of Surgical Technologists.

Earnings

As the shortage of registered nurses continues into the early 1990s, the need for qualified technicians should grow steadily.

In the early 1990s, the average starting salary for surgical technicians was $17,000 a year. Experienced technicians earned an average of $22,000 a year. Technicians working for the federal government earned starting salaries ranging from $14,000 to $23,000 per year.

Ways of getting more information

For more information write to the following:

► American Hospital Association
840 North Lake Shore Drive
Chicago, IL 60611

► American Medical Association
Division of Allied Health Education
and Accreditation
535 North Dearborn Street
Chicago, IL 60610

► Association of Surgical Technologists
8307 Shaffer Parkway
Littleton, CO 80127

Surveying and Mapping Technicians

Other Articles to Look At:

▶ **Archaeologists**
▶ **Cartographers**
▶ **Civil Engineering Technicians**
▶ **Civil Engineers**
▶ **Drafters**
▶ **Surveyors**

What surveying and mapping technicians do

The Egyptians employed surveyors to determine land holdings. The Romans used surveyors to map the principal roads of the Roman Empire. Today, surveyors help to establish property boundaries, lay out new communities, and establish the precise locations of new roads, bridges, dams and other structures. *Surveying and mapping technicians* help civil engineers, mapmakers, and professional surveyors determine, describe, and record geographic areas and features.

Surveying and mapping technicians work under the supervision of engineering professionals. These technicians are often responsible for setting up, adjusting, and taking readings from delicate surveying instruments. As these readings are taken, the technicians must keep careful field notes so that surveying reports will be accurate.

Surveying firms that employ surveying and mapping technicians often specialize in particular types of surveying work. Some firms do mostly land surveying. There technicians must be skilled in measuring property boundaries, reading maps, and interpreting land deeds. Preparing legal documents, such as deeds and leases, is also part of the technicians' work.

Technicians may also work for firms that do highway, pipeline, railway, or powerline surveying. *Geodetic surveying technicians* take measurements of large masses of land, seas, and space. This information helps others to set national boundaries and prepare maps.

Technicians who work for hydrographic surveying firms make surveys of harbors, rivers, and other bodies of water. These surveys help engineers to plan breakwaters, dams, locks, piers, and bridges.

Mining companies also use surveying and mapping technicians. These technicians use instruments that establish the boundaries of mining claims and also show features of the earth that indicate the presence of valuable ores.

Topographical surveying is another area where surveying technicians are employed. Topographical surveys establish the contours of the land. They show such features as mountains, lakes, forests, farms, and other landmarks. Technicians who do this type of surveying often take serial and land photographs with special cameras that photograph large areas of land. Such photographs allow accurate measurements to be made of land where roads, railway lines, and other engineering projects are planned.

Education and training

Surveying and mapping is highly technical work. A high-school diploma is a must. Students should take college preparatory classes that include all of the mathematics, science, and communications courses available. Courses in mechanical drawing and drafting are also helpful.

After high school, students should enroll in a junior college or technical school that offers training in surveying and mapping. These programs usually last two years and often include summer field study. Surveying firms often provide additional on-the-job training.

Earnings

Starting salaries for surveying and mapping technicians range from $10,000 to $23,000 per year. The average starting salary is $17,000 a year. Technicians with three to five years experience in the field average $21,000 a year.

Ways of getting more information

For more information about a career as a surveying and mapping technician, contact:

▶ Accreditation Board for Engineering and Technology
   345 East 47th Street
   New York, NY 10017

▶ American Congress on Surveying and Mapping
   210 Little Falls Street
   Falls Church, VA 22046

▶ American Institute of Mining, Metallurgical, and Petroleum Engineers
   345 East 47th Street
   New York, NY 10017

▶ A surveying technician holds up a measuring pole so the surveyor at the other end can take distance and height measurements.

Surveyors

Other Articles To Look At:

▶ **Cartographers**
▶ **Civil Engineering Technicians**
▶ **Civil Engineers**
▶ **Geographers**
▶ **Geologists**
▶ **Surveying and Mapping Technicians**

What surveyors do

Surveyors use a variety of mechanical and electronic devices to measure exact distances and locate positions on the earth's surface. These geographical measurements are used in many ways—to determine property boundaries, for mapmaking, and in construction and engineering projects. Whenever it is necessary to establish exact locations and measure points, surveyors make an accurate and detailed survey of the area.

Exactly what surveyors do depends on their area of expertise and the type of job they are working on. Some work on proposed construction projects such as highways, airstrips, housing developments, and bridges to provide the necessary measurements before the engineers and construction crews begin work. Some help mapmakers chart unexplored regions; others survey land claims, bodies of water, and underground mines; still others clear the right-of-way for water pipes, drainage ditches, or telephone lines. Some measure such large areas of land, sea, or space that the measurements must take into account the curvature of the earth; others use special photographic equipment installed in airplane or ground stations to chart areas that are hard to reach in person.

Whatever their area of specialization, surveyors must enjoy working outdoors in all sorts of weather, must be comfortable with the mathematics necessary to make exact measurements, must have the aptitude to work with a variety of mechanical and electronic measuring devices, and must possess the leadership qualities to direct and supervise the work of people in their surveying team.

Education and training

While a person can become a surveyor's helper with just a high-school diploma, the more technical and professional jobs require at least some college education. Junior colleges and technical schools offer courses, ranging from one to three years, that prepare students for positions as surveying technicians. Those who wish to become surveyors will need a bachelor's degree in surveying, civil engineering, or one of the physical sciences from an approved four-year college. And to advance in some of the more technical specialties, graduate study beyond a bachelor's degree is recommended.

All fifty states require that land surveyors making property and boundary surveys be licensed or registered. The requirements vary

▶ A surveyor checks the distance of an object.

from state to state but in general include a college degree, several years of experience, and the ability to pass a surveying examination. More and more, the trend is to require at least a bachelor's degree in engineering to be registered as a professional surveyor.

Earnings

The employment outlook in surveying through the early 1990s is expected to be fairly good. As the field becomes more technically sophisticated, however, applicants with have degrees will win the best positions.

In the early 1990s, the average salary for registered land surveyors was $28,500, though surveyors with the most education and experience could earn much more.

Ways of getting more information

School and public libraries should have books on the history and nature of surveying. A visit to a construction site where surveying is being done would give you a chance to talk with professional surveyors.

For more information about a career in surveying write to:

▶ American Congress on Surveying and Mapping
  210 Little Falls Street
  Falls Church, VA 22046

▶ American Society of Photogrammetry and Remote Sensing
  210 Little Falls Street
  Falls Church, VA 22046

Swimming-Pool Servicers

Other Articles to Look At:

▶ **Construction Workers**
▶ **General Maintenance Mechanics**
▶ **Heating and Cooling Mechanics**
▶ **Janitors and Cleaners**
▶ **Pipefitters and Steamfitters**

What swimming-pool servicers do

Swimming-pool servicers take care of swimming pools. They use a net with a long handle to remove leaves and trash from the water's surface. They clean the sides and bottom of the pool. To do so, they may use detergent, brushes, an underwater vacuum cleaner, hoses, and a sander. They use handtools to adjust and make minor repairs to the pool's pumping and heating equipment. They clean and repair the filter system.

Servicers also add chemicals to the water to purify it. Before doing so, they test the water to see which chemicals are needed. They are careful to add the correct amount of each chemical. If they add too little, they may not kill all of the germs in the water. After servicing a pool, these workers write a report of the work performed. A copy of this report is given to the pool owner. Another copy is kept for the company's files.

In areas with cold winters, outdoor swimming pools must be closed for the cold months. Servicers remove equipment such as ladders and diving boards. They put this equipment in storage. They drain the swimming pool and the filter. The pool may be covered with a large piece of waterproof canvas. Servicers check all of the equipment to see if anything needs to be fixed or replaced.

Opening a pool in the spring involves many tasks. Servicers take the canvas cover off the pool. If the owner wishes, they may paint the inside of the pool. They take the ladders and other equipment out of storage and install this equipment. They start the system and look for problems such as leaks. They make any necessary repairs. Servicers fill the pool and make sure that the heating and circulation system is working properly. Finally, they add the necessary chemicals to the water.

Swimming-pool servicers work for companies located throughout the country. Most servicers are employed by small companies. Larger companies may build and install pools in addition to servicing them.

Education and training

Swimming-pool servicers learn their skills on the job. They are trained by experienced employees. Many employers prefer workers with experience in construction, a high-school diploma, or both. Servicers must be licensed drivers, because they have to travel to the pools they service.

Earnings

The job outlook for swimming-pool servicers is good in the early 1990s. The number of swimming pools and hot tubs is growing. This will mean more work for servicers. Many servicers leave their jobs, or to find year-round jobs. This creates more job openings for new and experienced pool servicers.

After completing their on-the-job training, pool servicers have earnings that range from about $9,600 to more than $12,000 per year. Servicers who have special skills or who work quickly may earn more than other workers. Some servicers earn additional money by working part-time in swimming pool stores.

Ways of getting more information

The pool manager of a public or school pool may be able to help you contact a pool servicer.

For more information write to the following:

▶ National Spa and Pool Institute
2111 Eisenhower Avenue
Alexandria, VA 22314

▶ A swimming pool servicer nets debris that has blown into the pool during the night.

Switchboard Operators

Other Articles to Look At:

- ▶ **Hotel Clerks**
- ▶ **Mail Carriers**
- ▶ **Receptionists**
- ▶ **Telephone Operators**
- ▶ **Traffic Agents and Clerks**
- ▶ **Travel Agents**

What switchboard operators do

Switchboard operators handle the telephone calls that come into and go out of a business or office. There are two main types of switchboard operators: central office operators and PBX operators.

Central office operators work for a telephone company. They answer calls from people who want to know a phone number, or they connect calls that people want to make. Some of the operators in the central office are directory assistance operators. When someone calls asking for a person's number, they enter the name in a computer and the number appears on their screen. Central offices also employ long distance operators. They handle collect calls, overseas calls, and conference calls. Pay-phone calls also go through the long distance operator.

PBX stands for "private branch exchange." More than half of all switchboard operators are PBX operators. They work at the switchboards of private companies. When calls come into the company they answer them pleas-

antly, provide any information the caller may want, transfer calls to employees within the company, and take messages.

There are switchboard operators in many other areas. Operators in airports are called *communication center operators.* They page passengers and keep an eye on the airport's alarm system. *Police switchboard operators* take calls and pass information quickly to police officers. *Telephone answering services* have switchboard operators to take calls for people who pay to use the service.

Most switchboard operators work a standard forty-hour week. PBX operators usually work during regular business hours. Central office operators and those who work in 24-hour-a-day places such as hospitals and police stations may work evening or night shifts.

Education and training

Switchboard operators should have at least a high-school education. High-school courses in speech, mathematics, and business will be useful later as an operator. Telephone companies usually train their own operators on the job. New operators may be given several weeks of instruction before they begin on-the-job training. They learn how telephone switchboard equipment works and what the different telephone beeps and tones mean. They also listen to tapes of their own voices and practice to improve how they sound. Most private companies train their own PBX operators, too. Switchboard operators should have pleasant, friendly voices.

▶ Switchboard operators plug calls in to receiving phone lines.

Earnings

Job opportunities for central office operators are not expected to increase greatly throughout the early 1990s. This is because new electronic and computer equipment is taking over more and more tasks that people have done in the past. The outlook is better for PBX operators. Here, jobs regularly open up as operators move on to other employment. In the early 1990s, the starting salaries for central office operators fell between $12,000 and $24,000 a year. PBX operators earned a salary of $12,000 to $18,000 per year.

Ways of getting more information

For more information write to:

▶ American Society of Traffic and Transportation
PO Box 33095
Louisville, KY 40232

▶ International Brotherhood of Teamsters, Chauffeurs, Warehousemen and Helpers of America
25 Louisiana Avenue, NW
Washington, DC 20001

Systems Analysts

Other Articles to Look At:

▶ **Computer Operating Personnel**
▶ **Computer Programmers**
▶ **Engineers**
▶ **Mathematicians**
▶ **Scientific and Business Data-Processing Technicians**

What systems analysts do

Systems analysts help banks, government offices, and businesses of all kinds understand their computer systems. As more and more change from keeping records by hand to storing data in computers, analysts who can tailor computer systems and programs to the needs of a business, or even to the needs of just one department within a business, will become very important to any organization.

A system analyst for the personnel department of a large company would, for example, first talk with the manager about what areas the computer could help with. The manager might be interested in knowing about how a new policy of giving employees longer paid vacations at Christmas has affected company profit's for the month of December. The analyst can then show the manager what computer program to use, what data to enter, how to read the charts or graphs that the computer produces and so on. The work of the analyst thus frees the manager to review the raw data—in this case, the numbers that show company profits were the same as in the previous Decembers—and decide how this information should affect company policy.

Once analysts have the computer system set up and running, they then advise on possible equipment and programming changes. The areas analysts specialize in are as different as the businesses themselves; some deal with basic accounting while others help decide such complex questions as the flight path of a space shuttle.

Education and training

Almost all systems analysts have at least a bachelor's degree with majors in such subjects as computer science, mathematics, engineering, accounting, or business. Analysts going into specialized areas (aeronautics, for example) usually have graduate degrees as well.

In addition to a college degree, job experience as a computer programmer is very helpful. Many businesses hire systems analyst trainees from the ranks of their computer programmers. Systems analysts with several years experience are often permitted into managerial jobs, especially as businesses find they need top staff members with an understanding of computers.

Earnings

This field is one of the fastest growing, and companies are always looking for qualified analysts, especially those with graduate degrees in computer science. Analysts are often in good positions to bargain for higher salaries or more benefits.

Beginning yearly salaries for systems analysts are about $28,000 in the early 1990s. The average range of pay for experienced analysts was between $34,000 and $55,000. Salaries for analysts in government are somewhat less than the average for private industry.

Ways of getting more information

Many high schools offer classes in computer programming and this training helps in finding a part-time or summer job. Banks and insurance companies are often looking for students with some background in computers to work in data entry or programming while still in high school or college.

For more information write to the following:

▶ Two systems analysts discuss the information path on a flow chart for their computer system.

▶ American Federation of Information Processing Societies
1899 Preston White Drive
Reston, Va 22091

▶ Association for Systems Management
24587 Bagley Road
Cleveland, OH 44138

▶ Data Processing Management Association
505 Busse Highway
Park Ridge, IL 60068

Taxidermists

Other Articles to Look At:

▶ **Archaeologists**
▶ **Artists**
▶ **Biologists**
▶ **Commercial Artists**
▶ **Museum Occupations**
▶ **Veterinarians**

What taxidermists do

Taxidermists prepare, stuff, and mount the skins of birds, animals, and fish to create life-like models. Some of these models are trophies for hunters. Others are created for museum exhibits.

Taxidermists begin their work by skinning the animal they are preparing. They do this work with special knives, scissors, and pliers. One the skin is removed, it is preserved with chemical solutions.

Then the taxidermists create a foundation meant to resemble the skeleton of the animal. The foundation is made with materials that include clay, plaster, burlap, papier mache, wire mesh, and glue. After the foundation has been created, the preserved skin is attached with adhesives or modeling clay. Finally, the eyes, teeth, and claws are attached. In the case of the eyes, taxidermists often use glass or plastic replicas because it is difficult to preserve the original tissue.

Taxidermists work with a variety of subjects including large game animals, such as elk and bears, birds, fish, and reptiles. Usually, taxidermists create a model of the entire animal. Sometimes, however, they only model the head. This is often true of large animals, especially those with impressive antlers. And sometimes taxidermists will only preserve the skin of an animal. Such skins are often used as rugs.

Museums often call on taxidermists to create models of animals that are extinct. In such cases, the taxidermists work from detailed drawings and paintings of animals. They use natural and artificial furs, teeth, claws, and feathers to create a model that looks as much as possible like the extinct animal must have looked. Natural science museums also use taxidermists to create the dioramas with animals in their habitats.

Animals are donated or obtained from zoos, parks, or other places when the animal dies from natural causes. After the veterinarian determines the cause of death, the taxidermist comes in to prepare the animal for display.

The animal is set in a display with a wall painting behind it and plants and other items around it that would be found in its home in nature. This creates a sense of what the animal's natural environment is, and for rare animals, this may be the only chance most people get to see it.

Education and training

Taxidermists must have artistic ability, a good knowledge of animal anatomy, and special

▶ A taxidermist fills a fish with stuffing to keep the fish's shape.

training in taxidermy processes. High-school students should take courses in art, biology, and wood and metal shop. After high school, students can attend one of eight schools in the United States that offer courses in taxidermy.

Earnings

Beginning taxidermists often earn just the minimum wage. Experienced taxidermists average about $14,000 per year. Museum workers may earn $20,000 a year or more, but they usually have other duties in addition to their taxidermy work.

Ways of getting more information

You can get more information about a career as a taxidermist by writing to the following:

▶ American Institute of Taxidermy
3232 McCormick Drive
Janesville, WI 53545

▶ Fin, Feather, Fur School of Taxidermy
515 DuPree Drive
Jacksonville, AR

▶ National Taxidermists Association
18626 St. Clair Avenue
Cleveland, OH 44110

▶ North American Institute of Taxidermy
2408 Penn Avenue North
Minneapolis, MN 55411

▶ Southland School of Taxidermy
2603 Osceola Street
Baton Rouge, LA 70805

Taxi Drivers

Other Articles to Look At:

▶ **Automobile Mechanics**
▶ **Bus Drivers**
▶ **Delivery Drivers**
▶ **Industrial Truck Operators**
▶ **Toll Collectors**
▶ **Truck Drivers**

What taxi drivers do

Taxi drivers take passengers from one place to another, charging a specified fee based on the length of travel and time as recorded on a device known as a taximeter.

In addition to taking people from one place to another, taxi drivers may help passengers with their luggage, pick up and deliver packages, and provide sight-seeing tours for visitors to a city. They must be familiar with the best routes to get from place to place, must be able to get along with the many different people who ride in their cabs, and must drive well and safely in heavy traffic and in all kinds of weather.

Taxi drivers may either own their own cabs, rent cabs, or drive company-owned cabs. In any case, they must keep accurate records of the passengers they deliver and the fees they collect.

Taxi drivers get their passengers, or "fares," in several different ways. Most cabs have two-way radio systems through which drivers are notified by a dispatcher as to where to pick up passengers. Others pick up fares at cab stands to which they return after delivering each passenger. Still others park near airports or other buildings where there are many prospective passengers, such as hotels, theaters, restaurants, etc. And, of course, taxi drivers may pick up passengers as they drive the city streets. Most work long hours (including weekends, nights, and holidays), and though they enjoy a certain amount of independence, they must develop considerable self-discipline, since their earnings are dependent on their fares.

Education and training

No formal education is necessary to become a taxi driver, though applicants would do well to have at least an eighth-grade education. The main requirements are that drivers be in good health, have a good driving record, and no criminal record. Most large cities require that taxi drivers have a special taxicab operator's license in addition to a chauffeur's license. These licenses are issued by police departments, safety departments, or public utilities commissions and usually require both a driving and a written examination.

Earnings

There is a high turnover rate in this occupation, creating a steady number of openings. In large cities, getting an owner's license for an independent taxi can be expensive and difficult. Interested people should keep in mind

▶ A taxi driver waits for a passenger to return to the cab.

that most of these openings will be in large metropolitan areas, however, as people in small towns and suburbs generally drive their own cars and don't need the services of taxicabs as much.

In the early 1990s, full-time taxi drivers averaged between $15,600 and $31,200 annually. Most worked eight to ten hours a day, five or six days a week, and the tips they received for good service generally came to 15 to 20 percent of their total income.

Ways of getting more information

The best way to find out about the rewards and responsibilities of driving a taxi is to ride in a cab and talk to the driver in person. Learning to drive well and safely through a high-school drivers' education course is also good preparation.

For more information about job opportunities in your area, contact local cab companies or the local office of the state employment service.

Tax Preparers

Other Articles to Look At:

▶ **Accountants**
▶ **Auditors**
▶ **Banking Credit Analysts**
▶ **Bookkeepers**
▶ **Insurance Policy Processing Occupations**

What tax preparers do

Tax preparers fill out tax forms and help people figure out how much money (if any) they owe in taxes. They use their knowledge of local, state, and national tax laws to ask tax-related questions, analyze important tax documents and then complete tax returns for individuals and business firms.

To fill out tax forms, preparers meet with clients privately and look over all important tax documents. Preparers need to see wage statements, records of other income (like interest on a bank account), and any property tax information. Preparers often like to see a copy of the previous year's tax return. For most clients, especially business clients, it is also important to have an accurate listing of all business expenses. (Many business expenses are tax-deductible.) Preparers then talk to the client to get additional information concerning their financial situation. They may ask questions about a client's investments or get details on how much the client spent on a business trip. Preparers must also be aware of any unusual profits or losses in a particular year. It is important to know, for example, if a client had large medical expenses or a great increase in the value of his or her stocks.

Once the financial information has been collected, tax preparers figure out how much taxes are owed and fill out the appropriate forms. If the tax return is relatively simple, the preparer will complete the return while the client waits. For more difficult returns (those requiring more calculations), the preparer will complete the forms at a later time.

Tax preparers must be very careful when doing tax calculations and determining what deductions a client is eligible for. Preparers use calculators and computers to check their results, and tax forms are always reviewed by another tax preparer to make sure they are accurate. Tax preparers must sign every tax form they complete and give a copy of the completed form to the client. Preparers always keep a record of all completed tax forms.

Tax preparers who work for tax service firms are often called *tax interviewers*. Most of their clients come to them during "tax season" between January and mid-April. There are also a large number of tax preparers who are self-employed and work out of their homes.

Preparers must keep up with any changes in local, state, or federal tax laws. This requires constant study. Many tax companies sponsor review sessions each year during which time important tax law changes are discussed.

Education and training

Preparers must be able to work under deadline pressure and be able to work with nervous or upset clients. The process of filling out tax forms can be very stressful for some clients and preparers must be able to handle these situations with tact and calm.

Although there are no specific educational requirements for this job, all preparers are high-school graduates and most have at least some college training. Many preparers earn a college degree in business administration with an emphasis on taxation.

Most tax services provide new workers with on-the-job training during which time a new employee is carefully supervised. The new worker may spend several weeks or months reviewing the work of other preparers before seeing clients. Most preparers have at least some work experience before starting their own tax-preparation business.

Earnings

As tax laws continue to become more complicated, more people will use the services of tax preparers. This should lead to good job opportunities for those in this field. Because most people need assistance between January and April of each year, many of these jobs will be part-time. During the tax season preparers may work seven days a week, eleven hours a day.

Earnings depend on how many tax returns a preparer can complete. Preparers can expect to earn between $50 and $150 a return depending on how complicated the return is. Those who work for a tax service may have a set salary and get paid extra for each return they complete.

▶ A tax preparer checks a client's records while filling in the client's tax return forms.

Ways of getting more information

A good way to find out if you would enjoy being a tax preparer is to take a course in tax preparation or interview a preparer already working in the field.

In addition, write to the following organization and ask for information about being a tax preparer:

▶ National Association of Tax Practitioners
1015 West Wisconsin Avenue
Kaukauna, WI 54130

Teacher Aides

Other Articles to Look At:

▶ **Childcare Workers**
▶ **Elementary School Teachers**
▶ **Kindergarten Teachers**
▶ **Recreation Workers**
▶ **Secondary School Teachers**

What teacher aides do

Teachers must plan lessons, teach grade papers, prepare exams, attend faculty meetings, and perform other duties around the school. *Teacher aides* take care of some of the more routine school tasks and thus free the teacher to spend more time preparing for and teaching classes.

The duties of a teacher aide include preparing some instructional materials, helping students with classroom work, and supervising lunchrooms, playgrounds, and other areas around and within the school. Some teacher aides also do administrative paperwork, grade tests, and operate audiovisual equipment.

Some teacher aides work directly in the classroom. They may take attendance and distribute materials such as books, photocopies, and writing supplies. They also set up and operate slide and film projectors, tape recorders and phonographs, and VCRs.

Teacher aides also work outside of the classroom. They may be in charge of keeping order in the cafeteria, the library, hallways, and on the playground. They might also make sure students get on the correct school bus.

Teacher assistance is an important part of the teacher aides' job. Aides may help teachers by doing filing, typing, and photocopying. They may fill out request forms for classroom supplies. Teacher aides may even grade homework and tests that require objective answers—that is, definite right answers.

In some schools, teacher aides may even do some teaching. The aides may lecture, conduct group discussions, or listen to elementary school children read. Aides may take charge of school projects, such as science fairs. They may also take students on field trips.

Teacher aides work at all levels of education. Although they are most often found in elementary schools, teacher aides also work in high schools and even at some colleges and universities. At the college level, teacher aides are often graduate students.

Education and training

Educational requirements for teacher aides depend on the type of work the aides will be doing. Teachers aides who handle just clerical or supervisory duties may need only a high-school diploma. Sometimes, even a high-school education is not required. If the aides will be doing any teaching or classroom work, some college work is usually required. Sometimes a college degree is necessary.

Teacher aides often receive on-the-job training, usually under the supervision of a certified teacher.

▶ A day care worker teaches children how to prepare a snack.

Earnings

The need for teachers aides is expected to increase about as fast as average during the early 1990s. The relatively high turnover in this career should result in openings to replace those workers who leave the field.

Salaries for teacher aides vary with geographic location, the academic qualifications of the aide, and the duties performed. Teacher aides performing nonteaching duties usually earn about $6.00 an hour. Aides with some teaching duties average about $6.40 an hour.

Ways of getting more information

Interested students can get more information about career as a teacher aide by writing to the following:

▶ American Federation of Teachers
555 New Jersey Avenue NW
Washington, DC 20001

Technical Writers

Other Articles to Look At:

▶ **Computer Programmers**
▶ **Editors**
▶ **Radio and Television Announcers**
▶ **Writers**

What technical writers do

Technical writers put scientific and technical information into easily understandable language. They prepare service manuals, sales literature, catalogs, and other instructional materials used by sales people to sell various types of equipment. This instructional material is also used by technicians who install, maintain, and repair the equipment. Many writers develop instructional guides for users of home computers. Occasionally, technical writers assist in the preparation of speeches, articles, and other scientific papers.

Before technical writers begin a project, they must have a thorough understanding of the subject they are writing on. Before creating literature on a computer system or other product, for example, they study reports, journal articles, engineering drawings, and other materials that explain in detail how a product is built and how it works. Writers also talk to engineers, scientists, and other specialists who have a good background in the development of a particular product. After this research, the writer might observe the product being made to see firsthand how the various parts are put together.

After collecting enough background information, the writer is ready to begin writing. A service manual will often require more detail than a sales catalog, but all materials require a clear writing style that fully explains how a product works. Some writers arrange for the preparation of graphs, charts, and other artwork to illustrate how a product works.

After a first draft has been prepared, the technical writer will ask engineers and other people familiar with the product to read the material to check if it is accurate and understandable. The engineers' comments help the writer find out if there is a need for additional information or to change the style or content of the material.

Education and training

Technical writers must be able to express their ideas clearly and logically. They should be able to present the information in a creative way and also have the discipline to complete a project on time. Writers should be familiar with research techniques and have an understanding of how computers operate.

Most technical writers start their careers as scientists, engineers, or technicians. Some writers begin as research assistants in a company's technical information department. The best way to become a technical writer is to have a bachelor's degree in a specialized field

▶ Technical writers confer with the scientist on how to best explain an aspect of the work the scientist is doing.

such as engineering or business. Courses in English and writing are also helpful.

Earnings

Because of the increasing need to communicate scientific and technical information to sales people, researchers, and others, technical writers should find excellent job opportunities in the early 1990s. But, as is the case with all jobs in the writing field, there will be a great deal of competition for these jobs.

The average salary is between $22,000 and $30,000 per year; those with many years of experience should $40,000 or more annually.

Ways of getting more information

A good way to find out if you would enjoy being a technical writer is to work on a school newspaper or gain other writing experience.

In addition, write to the following:

▶ Society for Technical Communication
815 15th Street, NW
Washington, DC 20005

▶ Women in Communications
PO Box 17460
Arlington, VA 22216

Telecommunications Technicians

Other Articles to Look At:

▶ **Cable-Television Technicians**
▶ **Communications Equipment Mechanics**
▶ **Electronics Technicians**
▶ **Telephone Installers and Repairers**

What telecommunications technicians do

Telecommunications technicians install, maintain, and repair a wide variety of telecommunications equipment. Telecommunications equipment is used for transmitting voices and data across distances. Telecommunications systems are typically used to link telephones, but they may also link computers, fax machines, or teletype machines. Most telecommunications technicians work in telephone company offices or wherever telephone customers need equipment installed or repaired.

Other kinds of equipment are also used in telecommunications. Messages and signals can be sent using telegraph wires, laser beams, microwave transmissions, satellites, and fiber optics cables. Often several kinds of equipment are linked together in a complicated system. The following paragraphs describe a few of the many technicians who work in this complex industry.

Central office technicians or *switching equipment technicians* work in telephone company central offices. They install, test, repair, and maintain the equipment that automatically connects lines when customers dial.

PBX systems technicians work on PBXs or private branch exchanges, which are direct lines that businesses install to bypass phone telephone company lines. PBX equipment can provide specialized services like electronic mail and automatic routing of calls at lowest possible cost.

Submarine cable equipment technicians work with machines and equipment used to send messages over underwater cables. Working in cable offices and stations, they check on transmitters and printers and replace faulty parts.

Automatic-equipment technicians work for telegraph companies, maintaining and adjusting telegraph equipment.

Network control technicians work with electronic networks for transmitting data that use several different kinds of equipment, such as a combination of telephone lines, satellites, and computers. They electronically test the various parts of the network and monitor its performance in operation.

Microwave technicians help design, test, and install various parts of microwave communications systems and radar equipment. Most of these technicians are employed by the armed forces or defense industries.

Education and training

Telecommunications employers prefer to hire technicians who have already learned the necessary skills. Technicians can learn skills either through service in the military or from a post–high-school training program, such as those available at community and junior colleges or vocational institutes. These schools offer programs in telecommunications technology, computer maintenance, electronics, and other appropriate subjects.

While in high school, students who are thinking about entering this field should take computer courses, mathematics through algebra and geometry, and physics. They should take shop courses that introduce them to principles of electricity and electronics. They should also take English courses that help to develop language skills needed for reading instructional manuals and writing reports.

Earnings

The outlook for telecommunications technicians is mixed. Increasing computerization in the telephone industry is expected to greatly reduce the need for technicians who provide routine maintenance and repair services. On the other hand, employment in some areas of telecommunications is growing as computer technology changes and as equipment becomes increasingly complex. The demand for qualified microwave technicians, for example, should be very strong for the foreseeable future. In general, technicians who have the best training will be best able to get good jobs as new technology emerges.

The earnings of telecommunications technicians vary widely depending on the nature of their duties, level of experience, geographical location, and their employer. The average annual starting salary for technicians with good training is usually between $19,000 and $25,000. After several years experience technicians can make about $30,000 to $35,000 a year or more.

▶ With the wiring from a major phone line hookup, a telecommunications technician adds a connector to the lines that sends calls to the main cable.

Ways of getting more information

With the help of a teacher or guidance counselor, students may be able to arrange a visit to a local telephone company to see technicians on the job and talk with them. A radio or electronics club can provide some firsthand experience in the kinds of tasks that technicians do.

In addition, students can write to the following organizations for more information:

▶ Communications Workers of America
1925 K Street, NW
Washington, DC 20006

▶ United States Telephone Association
900 19th Street, NW, Suite 800
Washington, DC 20006

Telemarketers

Other Articles to Look At:

► **Advertising Workers**
► **Marketing Researchers**
► **Public Relations Workers**
► **Receptionists**
► **Telephone Operators**

What telemarketers do

Telemarketers sell goods, services, and ideas on the telephone. They also take orders, handle complaints, and conduct surveys. Their skills at dealing with the public on the phone are of great use to many different kinds of businesses.

Many stores and manufactures have toll-free 800 numbers, and they encourage customers to use the phone to ask questions or make complaints. Some stores don't have retail outlets but instead sell all of their products through catalogs. Telemarketers take customers' calls as the come in, seven days a week, twenty-four hours a day.

Telemarketers are employed either by the firm selling the goods or services or by an agency that sells the services of its telemarketers for limited periods of time. Some agencies work in one particular field. For example, an agency may specialize in fundraising or in book or magazine promotions.

Telemarketers make outgoing calls and receive incoming calls. The outgoing calls are usually to persons who returned a reply card or who have shown some interest in a product. Sometimes telemarketers make "cold calls" to potential customers chosen at random. When telemarketers make those calls they usually deliver a prepared message.

Telemarketers who take inbound calls not only accept orders for various products but also do such other jobs as make airplane reservations, sell tickets to concerts or ballgames, and give out various kinds of information.

Many telemarketers work in offices, usually at the company or agency headquarters. They make their calls in an office with four or five other workers or in a room with several hundred. Some companies employ telemarketers who work out of their own homes, usually during the evening hours.

Education and training

Most telemarketing centers and agencies want persons with at least a high-school diploma, and some firms hire only college graduates. Classes that help prepare students for this field are speech, drama, English, and business.

Telemarketers usually receive a great deal of on-the-job training. Companies or agencies that hire telemarketers have instructors on their staffs who show new employees how to use the equipment and how to read the scripts. They teach them sales techniques and listening skills. Instructors advise trainees on how to calm angry customers and how to respond to complaints.

▶ A telemarketer calls one of the people on her contact list.

Those who would like to go into this field should have patience and, especially, a good attitude. Telemarketers may deal often with rude customers, and they must always remain courteous.

Earnings

Telemarketing is a booming field in the early 1990s. Many companies have realized that selling their products over the phone is as effective as person-to-person sales and much less expensive.

The salaries earned depend on what kind of calls are being made. In the early 1990s, part-time employees making simple calls earn between minimum wage and $8.00 per hour. Telemarketers making business-to-business calls can make between $17,000 and $30,000 per year.

Ways of getting more information

For more information write to the following:

▶ American Marketing Association
   250 South Wacker Drive, Suite 200
   Chicago, IL 60606

Telephone Installers and Repairers

Other Articles To Look At:

▶ **Communications Equipment Mechanics**
▶ **Electrical Technicians**
▶ **Electricians**
▶ **Industrial Electronic Equipment Repairers**
▶ **Line Installers and Cable Splicers**
▶ **Telecommunications Technicians**

What telephone installers and repairers do

Telephone installers and repairers put in, take out, service, and repair telephones in homes and offices. Whenever customers request a new telephone, add an extension, or replace an old wall telephone, installers do all the necessary work. They travel to the customer's home or office in a truck that contains all the needed equipment. If the customer needs a new connection to the central telephone office, installers climb a nearby telephone pole to attach the incoming wire to the service line. On some jobs, they bore through walls and floors to do the necessary wiring. In addition to home and business telephones, installers also put in telephone booths and coin collectors.

Sometimes wear and tear of wires and parts cause a telephone to work improperly. When this happens, it is the job of the telephone repairer to test the phone, locate the trouble, and fix the problem. Sometimes the jobs of telephone installer and telephone repairer are combined, and the worker is called a *telephone installer-repairer.*

Some stores, business offices, hotels, and so on, have a single telephone number. However, to channel the large number of incoming and outgoing calls they use a switchboard system. This is like having their own private telephone system (called a private branch exchange, or PBX) within the building. A *PBX installer* sets up the necessary wiring and switchboard equipment to make the system function. Some PBX installers also set up teletypewriters, mobile radiotelephones, and equipment for television and radio broadcasting. And, like regular telephone repairers, *PBX repairers* locate the trouble in and then repair PBX systems. The PBX installer-repairer combines the jobs of PBX installer and PBX repairer.

Education and training

Telephone companies like to hire inexperienced persons and train them for telephone and PBX installation and repair jobs. However, to be considered for a telephone training program, applicants must be high-school or vocational school graduates who like working with their hands and have a fair amount of mechanical ability.

Once hired, new workers must complete a seven-month training program that combines on-the-job work experience with formal classroom instruction. After workers have become

▶ A telephone installer checks the new telephone lines from the stadium press box.

qualified telephone installers, additional training is necessary before they can become telephone repairers, PBX installers, or PBX repairers.

Earnings

The volume of telephone service is expected to increase in the next decade, and interested persons should find many opportunities for steady work as telephone and PBX installers and repairers. However, technological changes are expected to limit the types and numbers of repairs needed, which could also limit employment possibilities somewhat.

In the early 1990s, the average annual salary for telephone and PBX installers and repairers was about $27,082. Salaries vary, however, with experience and geographic location.

Ways of getting more information

Librarians will be able to direct readers to material about the history and nature of the communications industry. Building electronic kits or putting together model airplanes or cars are ways to test your mechanical inclinations and ability to work with your hands and follow drawings and plans.

For more information write to:

▶ Communications Workers of America
  1925 K Street, NW
  Washington, DC 20006

▶ International Brotherhood of Electrical Workers
  1125 15th Street, NW
  Washington, DC 20005

Telephone Operators

Other Articles to Look At:

▶ **Hotel Clerks**
▶ **Radio and Telegraph Operators**
▶ **Receptionists**
▶ **Reservation and Transportation Ticket Agents**
▶ **Travel Agents**

What telephone operators do

Telephone operators customers complete telephone calls and answer customer inquiries for telephone numbers, twenty-four hours a day and seven days a week. They may also help customers who have difficulty in dialing or those in emergency situations.

Telephone company operators usually work in large central offices. They wear headsets that contain both an earphone and a microphone, leaving their hands free to operate the switchboard, or, more often now, the computer terminal in front of which they are seated. Operators provide customers with a variety of services. They help customers with collect calls, long-distance calls, and other connections that require assistance. In these instances, they obtain the information needed to complete the call and record the details for billing. Directory assistance operators obtain telephone numbers for customers by using telephone directories that have alphabetical and geographical listings. Upon finding the telephone number, the directory assistance operator will read the number to the customer, or will activate a computerized recording that provides the customer with the number.

Although most people are familiar with the operators that work for telephone companies, there are also operators that work for large companies. These operators, called PBX operators, transfer incoming calls to the correct person, give information to callers, assist employees in making calls, and record charges for outgoing calls.

Education and training

Telephone operators should be pleasant, courteous, and have nice speaking voices. They should also not mind sitting for long periods of time. Operators must also be good listeners and have good reading skills and legible handwriting. Good hand-eye coordination and an ability to work under pressure are also important.

There are no specific educational requirements for this job, but most employers prefer to hire high-school graduates. New operators are given one to three weeks of individual training under the supervision of an experienced operator. During this time they are taught how to handle the different types of calls and any emergency situations. Operators are then assigned to a regular position at the switchboard. They continue to receive on-the-job training as more modern equipment becomes available.

▶ Telephone operators check telephone number listings on computers.

Earnings

Although telephone operators will continue to find fairly good job opportunities in the near future, computers and other types of automated equipment will decrease the number of operators needed. Private companies will continue to hire a large number of PBX operators but large telephone companies may reduce the number of operators they hire.

The wages paid to operators vary from state to state and even from city to city. The average yearly income is usually between $15,000 and $23,000. Those who work for telephone companies usually belong to unions and earn somewhat more than those who work for private companies.

Ways of getting more information

A good way to find out if you would enjoy being a telephone operator is to get a part-time or summer job as a telephone operator.

In addition, write to the following:

▶ Communications Workers of America
   1925 K Street, NW
   Washington, DC 20006

▶ United States Telephone Association
   900 19th Street, NW, Suite 800
   Washington, DC 20006

Testing Technicians

Other Articles to Look At:

► **Career Counselors**
► **Employment Counselors**
► **Guidance Counselors**
► **Psychologists**
► **Social Workers**

What testing technicians do

Testing technicians are workers who help give tests to people. The tests are often designed to measure a person's educational level, psychological condition, or occupational talents.

When they are giving a test, testing technicians give out blank test papers or sometimes testing equipment to the people being tested. They provide directions to the people and sometimes lead them through practice exercises. If testing equipment is involved, technicians demonstrate how to use the equipment.

While the test is in progress they watch the people who are taking the test to be sure that they follow all of the rules and directions of the test. This activity is usually referred to as "monitoring." Technicians also time the test, using a stop watch or electric timer, and they tell people when the time for the test is over.

After the test is over, technicians score the tests and record the results. To do this, they may use an answer sheet or some other kind of evaluation form.

Education and training

Testing technicians need to be at least high-school graduates. Once they are hired, technicians can expect to receive from three to six months of training that introduces them to the kinds of tests that they will be giving and the procedures for giving them.

While they are in high school, students who are interested in this field should be sure to take courses in mathematics and English. Their mathematics courses should cover such topics as handling fractions, computing ratios and percentages, and drawing and interpreting bar charts. Their English courses should prepare them to write reports with proper spelling, grammar, and punctuation. Testing technicians are often required to perform general clerical tasks, so students should also try to take courses that help to develop office skills. Other courses that will be of value include those that familiarize the student with computers and those that introduce the social sciences, such as psychology, sociology, or economics.

Earnings

The job outlook for testing technicians is difficult to predict. Job opportunities in public agencies, such as school districts or state employment offices, will vary from state to state. In some states, public agencies are facing reductions in the amount of money they have to spend, and they are forced to employ fewer people than they have in the past. In these states it may be very difficult to find a job as a testing technician.

Employment opportunities in private companies also vary from one area to another. In those regions with a strong economy, opportunities should be good. In places with weaker economies, jobs in this field will be harder to find.

The earnings of testing technicians vary widely depending on their levels of training, experience, and responsibility. Most earn somewhere between $12,000 and $20,000 a year. Some technicians with little training or experience may make only around $9,000 a year, while others with experience and special training may earn as much as $28,000 a year or more.

Ways of getting more information

Perhaps the best way to learn more about this job is to talk to a school guidance counselor. This person can explain about the kinds of tests that are often given to people and can probably provide information about the kinds of jobs available in educational, psychological, and occupational testing.

In addition, students may write for more information from any of the following organizations:

▶ A testing technician gives a practice test to a student to explain how the testing procedure works.

▶ American Association for Counseling and Development
5999 Stevenson Avenue
Alexandria, VA 22304

▶ American Psychological Association
1200 17th Street, NW
Washington, DC 20036

▶ American Society for Personnel Administration
606 North Washington Street
Alexandria, VA 22314

Textile Technicians

Other Articles to Look At:

▶ **Fashion Designers**
▶ **Industrial Engineers**
▶ **Quality-Control Technicians**
▶ **Manufacturers' Sales Representatives**
▶ **Textile Workers**

What textile technicians do

Textile technicians work with engineers and designers to make cloth, clothing, and other cloth products. Blankets and automobile seat belts, parachutes and bandages are all made of textiles. This field splits into two industries, the textile industry, which produces cloth, and the apparel industry, which produces clothing. Technicians are also called *apparel manufacturing technicians.*

In the textile industry, some technicians work on developing new kinds of yarn or thread. They work with natural fibers, such as wool or cotton, and with manmade materials, such as rayon. Sometimes they take a piece of fabric and figure out what fibers are in it and how it was made. Then they can decide how to improve it. For example, textile technicians have helped make flame-resistant cloth for fire fighters' coats and bacteria-resistant cloth for hospital gowns.

Both textile and apparel technicians may work in manufacturing. These technicians need to understand the complicated machines that carry out many manufacturing processes. They need to learn management and speaking skills so that they can train workers to operate machines. They may program computers to operate some machines.

They have to know how long each step of production takes, exactly what material is needed, and how the product will move from one process to another. For example, an apparel manufacturing technician may have to plan the cutting of fabric into pieces or the sewing of those pieces into a garment.

Other textile and apparel technicians work in laboratories testing the quality of the manufactured goods. These quality control technicians test cloth for strength, thickness, wrinkle resistance, color, and other things. In the apparel industry, technicians check garments for size, construction, and appearance.

Education and training

Textile technicians need to complete high school and take at least two years of further training at a technical school or a community college. High-school students interested in becoming textile technicians should study English, at least two years of mathematics, and science courses that involve laboratory work. Courses in computers and mechanical drafting will also be useful.

Two-year degree programs will include science, mathematics, English, and computer programming. Students who are interested in the textile industry will learn about different fibers, the processes of making yarn and fab-

▶ Two textile technicians register the color of each strand to be weaved into a cloth on a machine weaver.

ric, and methods of testing textiles. Apparel manufacturing technicians will learn about garment patterns, cloth-cutting, and management.

Earnings

Overall growth in the textile industry will be slow; however, the demand for technicians who know to work with computers and advanced machinery will increase.

Beginning textile technicians earn between $14,000 and $20,000. With four to six years of work experience, textile technicians earn up to $25,000 a year. Jobs in the apparel industry pay somewhat more than jobs in the textile industry. With increased experience and responsibility, technicians' salaries can go up to $40,000 or more.

Ways of getting more information

Visiting a textile or apparel factory, if there are any nearby, would be a good way to learn about how cloth or clothing is made.

For more information write to:

▶ American Apparel Manufacturers Association
   2500 Wilson Boulevard
   Arlington, VA 22201

▶ American Textile Manufacturers Institute
   1801 K Street, NW
   Washington, DC 20006

▶ National Council for Textile Education
   PO Box 391
   Charlottesville, VA 22902

Textile Workers

Other Articles to Look At:

▶ **Industrial Machinery Mechanics**
▶ **Knit Goods Industry Workers**
▶ **Leather Tanning and Finishing Workers**
▶ **Machinists**
▶ **Textile Technicians**

What textile workers do

Many of the products we use, from the clothes we wear to the rugs we walk on are made from textiles (woven fabrics). *Textile workers* are the ones involved with converting natural and manufactured fibers into usable products. Some workers operate machinery that makes the fiber and yarn used to produce fabrics while others are employed in the areas of design, research, and marketing. A worker's specific responsibilities depend on the area in which he or she works.

The textile manufacturing process begins with the preparation of manufactured or natural fibers for spinning. Operators oversee machines that break up large quantities of fibers, remove some of the damaged fibers, and blend the rest of the fibers together into spools of yarn. This yarn is then fastened onto other machines where it is woven together with other fabric to produce various products. While the machines are in operation, operators replace spools of yarn as needed and watch for any problems, such as yarn breaking or new needles needing to be put on.

Workers are also needed in other areas of the production process. They clean and wash the fabric after it has gone through the spinning machines and many fabrics are dyed with color or given special finishes that make them waterproof or wrinkle-resistant.

After the production process, workers inspect the fabrics to make sure there are no flaws, press the material so it has a "new" look, and box the material for shipping.

Other workers involved in the textile industry include the designers, who create patterns and then choose the colors and yarn to make those patterns; production managers, who supervise the making of the garments and keep track of costs and other important work records; and machine repair personnel, who fix any major problems and do maintenance tasks such as greasing and oiling the machines to prevent problems from occurring.

Education and training

The best way to become a worker is to complete an apprenticeship program offered by textile manufacturers. These programs range from several months to several years in duration and combine on-the-job training with courses in mathematics and machine shop practice. Many community colleges and technical schools also offer two-year programs in textile making.

▶ Watching a bolt of material being printed, a textile worker checks for quality of the design printed on the material.

Earnings

With the increased use of automated machinery and the increased competition from foreign textile companies, employment opportunities for textile workers should decline during the early 1990s. Most of the new workers will be hired to replace those who retire or stop working for other reasons.

The average salary for production workers is about $14,000 per year. Those who work late evening shifts may earn somewhat more than this. Supervisors and other managerial personnel should earn about $20,000 annually.

Ways of getting more information

For further information write to:

▶ American Textile Manufacturers Institute
  1801 K Street, NW
  Washington, DC 20006

▶ National Council for Textile Education
  PO Box 391
  Charlottesville, VA 22902

Tire Technicians

Other Articles to Look At:

▶ **Plastics Products Manufacturing Workers**
▶ **Plastics Technicians**
▶ **Quality-Control Technicians**
▶ **Rubber Goods Production Workers**

What tire technicians do

Tire technicians work for tire companies, testing tires to find out how strong the tires are, how long they will last, and whether or not there are any flaws in their construction. Sometimes they test experimental models of tires that are not yet ready for manufacturing, and sometimes they test samples of regular tires as they come out of the factory. Technicians who are involved mostly with testing tires from the factory are called *quality-control technicians.*

To do testing, tire technicians inflate the tires and mount them on machines that re-create the stresses of actual road conditions, such as traveling at high speeds, carrying heavy loads, or going over bumpy roads. The technicians can adjust the machines to change the speed or the weight of the load or the bumpiness of the road surface. Then, either while the tire is on the machine or after it is taken off, they use pressure gauges and other devices that detect whether any parts of the tire are damaged. They continue testing the tire until it fails or until it has lasted for some specified period of time.

Another kind of testing that tire technicians do involves cutting cross-sections from brand-new or road-tested tires. Technicians use power saws to cut up tires and then inspect the pieces for the condition of the cords, the plies (which are rubbery sheets of material inside the tire), and the tread.

Throughout the testing, tire technicians keep careful records of all test results. Later they prepare reports that sometimes include charts, tables, and graphs to help describe and explain the results of the tests.

Education and training

Tire technicians need to be high-school graduates. For some jobs, employers prefer applicants who have training in a field related to manufacturing or product-testing. This kind of training may be received at a vocational school or a community or junior college.

While in high school, students interested in this career should take courses in science and mathematics, including algebra and geometry, and English courses that improve their reading and writing skills. They should also take shop or laboratory science courses that introduce them to measuring devices, electrical machinery, and electronic testing equipment.

Earnings

Future employment opportunities for tire technicians are hard to predict. Employment levels in the tire industry are very much tied to the number of new cars being sold, and it is possible that the number of new cars manufactured and sold in this country will decrease in coming years. In addition, tiremakers in this country face competition from foreign tire manufacturers, so that production in this country could decline. It that happens, there will be fewer jobs for tire technicians.

Salaries for tire technicians vary depending on the kind of testing they do, how much supervision they require, and how much training they have. Some skilled and experienced technicians who can work with little supervision earn $30,000 to $36,000 a year or more. Technicians with little experience and no training after high school may make around $14,000 to $18,000 a year, although some may earn less. Most tire technicians make between $18,000 and $30,000 a year.

Ways of getting more information

Students can explore their interest in similar work through shop or laboratory science courses in which they operate machinery or make precise measurements with mechanical or electronic equipment.

In addition, students can write for more information from the following organizations:

▶ Checking the wear on the tire after a stress test, a technician measures the tread of a tractor tire.

▶ American Society for Quality Control
　　310 West Wisconsin Avenue
　　Milwaukee, WI 53203

▶ International Tire Association
　　PO Box 1067
　　Farmington, CT 06034

Title Searchers and Examiners

Other Articles to Look At:

▶ **Assessors and Appraisers**
▶ **Lawyers**
▶ **Legal Assistants**
▶ **Librarians**
▶ **Real Estate Agents and Brokers**
▶ **Underwriters**

What title searchers and examiners do

When a piece of real estate is sold, the buyer received title to it from the seller. Title is a legal right of ownership of property. But before title passes from the seller to the buyer, a title search and examination are usually done. This is the work of *title searchers* and *examiners.*

The purpose of a title search and examination is to make sure that the seller has clear title to the property. *Title searchers* begin by reading the search request. They find out what type of title evidence is required. They note the legal description of the property and the names of the people involved. Then, they begin the actual title search.

The title search is done using public and private records. These records list mortgages, deeds, and other legal documents that can effect the title to a property. They also compare the legal description in the title request with the one shown in the records. This allows time to check the deed of ownership and the description of the property's boundaries. Title searchers may request maps or drawings showing the boundaries of the property.

Title searchers also list transactions (business dealings) related to the property. For example, the owner may have hired a worker to install a new patio. If the owner did not pay the worker, he or she may have filed a lien against the property. A lien is a claim on property for an unpaid debt. Liens must be removed (paid off) to clear the title to a property. Title searchers also check tax records to make sure the owner has paid his or her taxes. If taxes are owed, they must be paid before clear title can pass to the new owner of the property.

Title examiners go over the information collected by title searchers. They decide whether the owner of a property has clear title to it. In doing so, they study copies of various records. Examines include mortgages, liens, and deeds. Examiners also check records of legal matters that can effect title to a property. These include births, marriages, and divorces. If the owner does not have clear title, examiners list what he or she needs to do to clear the title. Some title examiners work for title insurance companies. After they complete a title examination, they may prepare a title insurance policy. Such a policy guarantees that the seller has legal title to the property being sold.

Title searchers and examiners are employed by title insurance companies, government offices, and law firms.

▶ Title searchers check on property rights to a lot being purchased by a client.

Education and training
Title searchers are given on-the-job training. Most employers expect job seekers to have a high-school diploma. They look for people who can read quickly and who have clear handwriting.

It takes years of practical experience for a title examiner to become an expert in this field. Many title examiners have some college training. Subjects studies may include real estate law and business management.

Licenses or certificates are required for title searchers and examiners in some states.

Earnings
The job outlook for these workers is quite good. Jobs are most plentiful when the real estate market is strong.

Salaries of experienced title searchers range from $11,000 to about $15,000 per year.

Ways of getting more information
Although finding work in a title company's office may be difficult for a student, experience working in a bank or a real estate firm could be valuable.

For more information about the work of title searchers and title examiners write to:

▶ American Land Title Association
1828 L Street, NW, Suite 705
Washington, DC 20036

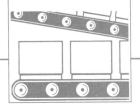

Tobacco Products Industry Workers

Other Articles to Look At:

▶ **Dairy Products Manufacturing Workers**
▶ **Plastics Products Manufacturing Workers**
▶ **Rubber Goods Production Workers**
▶ **Sporting Goods Production Workers**
▶ **Textile Workers**

What tobacco products industry workers do

Tobacco industry workers make cigars, cigarettes, chewing tobacco, smoking tobacco, and snuff. These products are made from leaf tobacco. Workers dry, cure, age, cut, roll, form, and package various products.

Workers first harvest the tobacco. Then the tobacco is cured or dried. Workers separate the tobacco leaves from the stems. This is done either by hand or by feeding the cured tobacco into machines. Then the tobacco is dried again by *redrying-machine operators* who use machines equipped with hot air and fans.

After redrying, the tobacco is aged by sprinkling it with water. *Bulkers* and *prizers* the pack, or prize, the tobacco into barrels called hogsheads. *Hydraulic-press operators* pack hogsheads using scales, electric hoists, and hydraulic presses.

After the tobacco has been aged, *blenders* mix together various kinds of tobacco to produce a mixture with certain characteristics. After blending, some tobacco is flavored with what is called "casing fluid." Casing workers prepare the fluid, soak the tobacco with it, and the remove the excess fluid.

Now the tobacco is ready to cut. Workers feed the tobacco into shredding machines. Some of the shredded tobacco is ground into a product called "snuff." Cut tobacco is fed into machines that manufacture cigarettes and cigars. Some cigars are made by hand. Machines also form tobacco into plugs, lumps, and twists. This type of tobacco is chewed. Workers then pack the tobacco products for shipping.

Also important to the tobacco industry are *product inspectors*. These workers are responsible for assuring the quality of tobacco products.

Education and training

No formal education is required for most tobacco products industry jobs. A grade school diploma is usually sufficient. Workers learn their skills on the job. Maintenance and mechanical workers may need a high-school diploma and machine maintenance experience or skills.

Earnings

Employment of tobacco industry workers is expected to remain steady in the early 1990s. However, because of the efforts of health

▶ At an auction, tobacco products industry workers examine different lots of tobacco produced.

care professionals Americans appear to be more aware of the health dangers of tobacco and as a result jobs in this industry are expected to slowly decline.

In the early 1990s, cigarette makers earned about $23,000 a year. Cigar workers earned less while skilled workers earned more. In general, salaries depend on plant size, plant location, and the level of the worker's skills.

Ways of getting more information

For more information about a career as a tobacco products industry worker write to the following:

▶ Bakery, Confectionery, and Tobacco Workers International Union
  10401 Connecticut Avenue
  Kensington, MD 20895

▶ Cigar Association of America, Inc.
  1100 17th Street, NW
  Washington, DC 20036

▶ Tobacco Growers' Information Committee, Inc.
  PO Box 18089
  Raleigh, NC 27619

▶ The Tobacco Institute
  1875 I Street, NW, Suite 800
  Washington, DC 20006

Toll Collectors

Other Articles to Look At:

▶ **Bank Tellers**
▶ **Car-Rental Agents**
▶ **Cashiers**
▶ **Counter and Retail Clerks**
▶ **Reservation and Transportation Ticket Agents**
▶ **Shipping and Receiving Clerks**

What toll collectors do

The U.S. economy depends on the huge, crisscrossing web of roads, bridges, and tunnels that spreads across the United States. Without this interconnecting system of transportation, people couldn't get to and from work, and goods couldn't get from farm to factory, or from stockroom to store. But the cost of building and maintaining the system is high, and many roads, bridges, tunnels, and even ferry boats charge a fee, or toll, to the people who use them. The workers who collect these fees are called toll collectors.

Toll collectors perform a wide range of duties. First and foremost, they collect tolls from vehicles passing through their toll stations. The rates vary according to the size or weight of the vehicle, so collectors must be aware of all the various rates possible. They make change, count and sort the money they receive, fill out bank deposit slips, and keep written records on the amount of traffic and kinds of vehicles that pass through their station.

In addition to handling the financial end of toll collecting, these workers give directions to travelers, pass on messages received through their radio equipment, and notify state police, ambulances, or other emergency services when necessary. They may monitor the automatic lanes at their stations (exact change lanes where motorists just toss their toll money into a basket), check for unsafe or prohibited vehicles on the roadway, and make sure the electronic, automatic, and other equipment at their station is working properly.

Toll collectors work around the clock, every day of the year. Their busiest shifts are usually on holidays, evenings, and weekends. Still, most collectors enjoy their work. They come in contact with all kinds of people every day, and have the satisfaction of knowing that their courtesy and friendliness give travelers a lasting impression of the thruway network as a whole.

Education and training

Toll collectors should have at least a high-school education, and those wishing to rise up the management ranks should have some college experience as well. People who have worked as cashiers will have an advantage over other applicants, but no previous training is required. All would-be collectors must take an exam before being hired, where they are tested on their ability to deal with the public,

▶ Toll collectors receive the money paid by drivers when they use a toll bridge or road.

make change and handle other financial transactions, and keep records and write reports.

Earnings

Salaries vary from state to state, but on the average beginning toll collectors earn about $11,500 a year, while more experienced collectors earn up to $19,000 a year. Those employees with the education, experience, and work skills to go into management may earn anywhere from $21,000 to $45,000 a year.

Ways of getting more information

Interested students can talk to people at the state job service office or toll authority about the exact responsibilities of toll collectors. Any experience in handling money and making change will also be valuable in this career.

For more information write to:

▶ American Association of State Highway and Transportation Officials
444 North Capitol Street, NW
Washington, DC 20001

▶ International Bridge, Tunnel and Turnpike Association
2120 L Street, NW, Suite 305
Washington, DC 20037

Tool and Die Makers

Other Articles to Look At:

▶ **Instrument Makers**
▶ **Machinists**
▶ **Molders**
▶ **Patternmakers**
▶ **Welders**

What tool and die makers do

Tool and die makers design and construct dies (metal forms) and other metal objects that are used in the manufacturing of car and airplane parts, refrigerators and other electrical machinery, and a variety of other products. They are highly skilled workers who drill and shape metal objects so that these objects can be used in the production of both large and small items. They work in automobile, airplane, and other metalworking industries.

Tool and die makers often work from rough sketches, verbal instructions, or blueprints. They sometimes work on parts that must not vary from specifications more than one ten-millionth of an inch. To meet these strict standards, tool and die makers use precision measuring devices and hand and power tools.

After determining how a part should be made, tool and die makers measure and mark the piece of metal that will be cut to form parts of the finished product. They then use grinders and other machine tools and hand-tools, such as files and chisels to cut or drill the metal as specified in the instructions. All metal parts must be carefully checked to make sure they meet the specifications. Tool and die makers use measuring instruments to keep a close check on dimensions through the production process. After being satisfied that all parts are correctly made, tool and die makers fit the pieces together to obtain the finished product.

Because tool and die makers work with high-speed machines, they must carefully follow safety rules and wear protective equipment. They always wear safety glasses for protection against bits of flying metal and often wear earplugs to lessen the impact of machine noise.

Education and training

Tool and die makers should have a strong interest in mechanical subjects and a superior ability to work with their hands. They should also be good at working with steel, metal, and other material and be skillful at using hand tools, power tools, and measuring devices. Tool and die makers spend most of the workday on their feet and are often required to lift or move heavy machinery; therefore workers should be in good physical condition.

Because tool and die makers often work alone or with little supervision, they must be resourceful people who start projects on their own. They should also be able to read engineering sketches and carefully follow instructions. Excellent vision is necessary, either with or without eyeglasses.

The best way to become a tool and die

maker is to complete a four-year apprenticeship. During the apprenticeship program, high-school graduates get on-the-job training in the use of machine tools and measuring instruments as well as classroom instruction in technical subjects such as mathematics, physics, and blueprint reading.

Some tool and die makers do not complete an apprenticeship program but rather start as machinists or machine tool operators and then become tool and die workers. Although these workers are already skilled in many of the measuring and cutting processes needed as a tool and die worker, they usually must have at least several months of close supervision before qualifying as tool and die makers.

▶ Using a small vice, a tool and dye manufacturer places a piece into the machine.

Earnings
Because of the increased use of automation in the manufacturing process, there will be limited opportunities for tool and die makers in the early 1990s. But, because of the many years required to become trained as a tool and die maker, those skilled in this field should find good job opportunities.

The average salary is about $30,000 per year. Apprentices start off earning about half this amount, but their pay is increased every six months, so that they are making nearly this amount by the end of their apprenticeship.

Ways of getting more information
A good way to find out about being a tool and die maker is to develop a hobby such as modelmaking or car repair that requires patience

and mechanical ability. It might also be possible to get a part-time or summer job at a machine shop and in that way learn more about the profession.

In addition, write to the following organizations and ask for information about being a tool and die maker:

▶ The National Tool Builders
   7901 Westpark Drive
   McLean, VA 22102

▶ The National Tooling and Machining
   Association
   9300 Livingston Road
   Fort Washington, MD 20744

Tour Guides

Other Articles to Look At:

▶ **Foreign-Service Officers**
▶ **Recreation Workers**
▶ **Reservation and Transportation Ticket Agents**
▶ **Teachers**
▶ **Travel Agents**

What tour guides do

Tour guides escort groups of travelers to different cities and countries. By acting as a link between the tourist and the area and its people they try to ensure that the trip will be as enjoyable and safe as possible.

The jobs performed by tour guides are varied. Some guides act as travel agents for the tour, booking airline flights or cruises or car rentals. They research area hotels and other lodgings and plan sightseeing tours. Guides try to meet the needs of the group by learning individual interests and needs. Older members of a tour, for example, may not want to climb fifty steps to visit a cathedral, and the tour guide would need to plan other activities for such travelers.

Many details can be worked out before the group leaves home. Hotel reservations, special exhibits, theater tickets, and side trips can all be booked weeks or months before the tour begins. But no matter how organized a tour guide is beforehand, many problems will arise during the trip, and guides must be able to act quickly and calmly to deal with them as they occur.

Guides must see that food and lodging meet expected standards and make sure all baggage and personal belongings are loaded on the plane or bus or train and that they are handled properly. Most importantly, tour guides must keep track of the people on their tours. It's their responsibility to see everyone gets home safely.

Tour guides are the sources of interesting information about the areas visited. They should be prepared to answer all kinds of questions, from details about local history to how to cash a traveler's check.

Education and training

College degrees are not necessary but are certainly helpful, especially if guides wish to lead tours to foreign countries. Courses in the history, art, and foreign languages, as well as in speech and communication, are very helpful.

Some large cities have professional schools that offer classes in becoming a travel agent. Community colleges may offer this training as well. Travel agencies and tour companies often provide their own training, which prepares guides to lead the tour packages they offer.

Earnings

Through the early 1990s growing needs for guides to conduct tours for business, recreation, education, and travel groups will exist.

▶ A tour guide explains water safety before taking a group on a river ride.

Many tour guides work only eight months, or fewer, out of the year. However, they may earn up to $15,000 for those months. Many guides earn weekly salaries that average $300 per week. Many are given gratuities by those on their tours. Guides receive their meals and accommodations free while conducting a tour; they also receive a daily stipend to cover personal expenses.

Ways of getting more information

Many large cities have zoos, theme parks, or historical districts and giving tours in any of them provides valuable experience on handling groups of people and giving brief lectures.

For more information write to:

▶ American Society of Travel Agents
  1101 King Street
  Alexandria, VA 22314

▶ Travel Industry Association of America
  1133 21st Street, NW
  Washington, DC 20036

Toxicologists

Other Articles to Look At:

▶ **Biologists**
▶ **Chemists**
▶ **Medical-Laboratory Technicians**
▶ **Pharmaceutical Technicians**
▶ **Pharmacologists**
▶ **Pollution-Control Technicians**

What toxicologists do

Toxicologists conduct research on toxic, or poisonous substances. They are concerned with detecting poisons; with discovering the effects of poisons on humans, plants, and animals; and with finding treatments for poisonous conditions.

Toxicologists work in many different situations. They may be part of a research team in a hospital or poison control center, where they work to help save emergency drug overdose victims or to solve long-term issues, such as the level of toxic material in cigarettes. They may work for a private company, such as a cosmetics firm, testing new products to determine the products' toxicity. They may work for government agencies concerned with protecting consumers from accidental exposure to poisons. For example, they might study fish to determine the level of mercury contained in them. Their results could be used by city, state, or federal officials to limit the level of mercury that man-ufacturing companies use in the manufacturing process.

Toxicologists keep careful records of all their research and then write reports on their findings. They may work with legislators to write new, protective legislation, on may appear at official hearings designed to discuss policy decisions. In all their work they must be conscientious, accurate, and patient; they must keep up to date on the most modern equipment and research procedures; and, since they deal with poisonous substances, they must pay the strictest attention to safety procedures.

Education and training

Many years of training are needed to become a toxicologist. Interested persons should have a doctorate in pharmacology, chemistry, or related science, with some post-doctorate work in toxicology as well. Today's toxicologist must also have a good working knowledge of computers, since much of the work involves sophisticated electronic equipment. Finally, all toxicologists must be licensed, though licensing requirements vary from state to state. Most licensing procedures include a check into the applicant's education, references, and work history, as well as a comprehensive written examination.

Earnings

Employment opportunities are expected to grow throughout the 1990s. As our society uses more and more chemicals and other toxins in agriculture and industry, there will be an increased need for trained professionals to determine and limit the health risks of these toxins. Job opportunities should be greatest in cities, as this is where most large hospitals and research facilities are located. As always, those with the most training and experience will win the best jobs.

As trained medical professionals, toxicologists earn very good salaries. Those with just a master's degree can expect to make $24,000 to $29,000 a year to start, while those beginning with a doctorate should earn between $30,000 and $50,000 per year. Experienced toxicologists can earn upwards of $80,000 a year.

Ways of getting more information

Ask your librarian for reading materials on the history and development of toxicology, or see if you can arrange a meeting with a practicing toxicologist at your local hospital or poison control center. Your science teacher can also direct you to journals and other reading material about this field.

For more information, writing to:

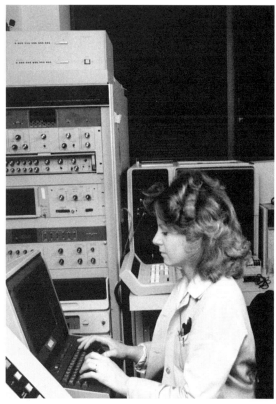

▶ Toxicologists test chemicals to determine if the compounds are harmful.

▶ American College of Toxicology
9650 Rockville Pike
Bethesda, MD 20814

▶ Society of Toxicology
1133 15th Street, NW
Washington, DC 20005

Toy Industry Workers

Other Articles to Look At:

▶ **Assemblers**
▶ **Designers**
▶ **Packaging and Paper Products Technicians**
▶ **Plastic Technicians**
▶ **Sporting Goods Production Workers**

What toy industry workers do

Toy industry workers put toys and games together. The toy industry makes all kinds of products including bicycles, video games, dolls, swing sets, puzzles, balls, and board games.

Some workers operate machines on assembly lines where each worker performs one step in making a toy. For example, some workers run machines that blow the filling into stuffed animals. Others run machines that put tires on the wheels of bicycles and tricycles. Workers may fill molds with plastic to shape the heads, arms, legs, and bodies of dolls and action figures. Other workers operate the machines that put these molded pieces together.

To make a game, some workers print the game board. Others use machines to cut out the cardboard backing and paste the game board on the backing. Some workers make only the dice for the games.

Some toy industry workers work with their hands to assemble toys. They may glue, clip, or nail pieces together. For example, puzzle assemblers put the pieces of a puzzle together. Some workers, called *hand finishers,* dress dolls or tie ribbons around the necks of stuffed animals.

When the toys are assembled, conveyor belts carry them to other workers who use machines to wrap and package them.

Toy industry workers work in factories. In a small factory, there may be one large area with about 200 workers all doing different things. Working in these factories is noisy. Some jobs require workers to stand most of the day. In most of these jobs, workers do the same thing over and over again; still, they must keep alert to see that each toy is made properly.

From July to September, many toy companies want their workers to work ten hours a day or longer to help get toys made for the holiday season. After September, toy companies slow down, some of them lay off their workers for part of the year. This means that some workers will have no work or no pay during the slow seasons.

Educations and training

There is no special education or training for toy industry workers. They learn on-the-job to operate the machines and do hand work. Reliable workers can become supervisors who train other workers and inspect their work. To help negotiate raises and better working conditions, toy industry workers can

▶ A toy industry work packs a game into its box before shipping.

join unions, such as the Amalgamated Toy and Novelty Workers.

Earnings

Because the demand for toys and games is growing, the need for workers will grow.

Many toy industry workers are paid hourly. Beginning workers earn the minimum wage. Experienced workers can earn $6.00 an hour or more. Workers who operate machines earn more than those who assemble toys by hand.

Some factories pay workers a certain amount for each toy they complete: this is called "piecework." The faster they work, the more pieceworkers can earn.

Ways of getting more information
Write for more information to:

▶ Industrial Designers Society of American
1142-E Walker Road
Great Falls, VA 22066

▶ Society of the Plastics Industry
1275 K Street, NW
Washington, DC 20005

▶ Toy Manufacturers of America
200 Fifth Avenue
New York, NY 10010

Traffic Agents and Clerks

Other Article to Look At:

▶ Billing Clerks
▶ Clerical Supervisors and Managers
▶ Industrial Traffic Managers
▶ Postal Clerks
▶ Service Sales Representatives
▶ Shipping and Receiving Clerks

What traffic agents and clerks do

Traffic agents and clerks are involved with the movement of cargo (goods) by air, water, truck, or rail. They handle the booking, billing, claims, and related paperwork for the movement of goods. They must understand how various laws effect their work. Examples of these laws include the Interstate Commerce Act, the Federal Trade Commission Act, and the Railways Labor Act.

These workers are employed by individual transportation companies. Their work differs from one kind of carrier to another.

Rate supervisors study rate and routes to find ways to reduce transportation costs. They supervise the work of *traffic clerks.* These clerks figure out the rates a company will charge for shipping goods of various kinds.

Freight rate analysts also study rates, as well as laws affecting transportation. They figure out how the company should charge its rates and practices. They also put together the company's rate manual.

Traffic managers direct other workers who deal with freight that is going out and coming in. Other traffic managers quote rates and give other information to customers. They also handle customer complaints about missing or damaged goods.

Traffic agents contact possible customers to try to get their freight business. They also contact travel agencies and other organizations to get passenger business. They call on possible customers to explain their company's services and the advantage of using them. Agents try to get shippers to agree to ship goods with their company. *Shipping services sales representatives* do similar work for package-delivery businesses.

Education and training

Most companies prefer traffic agents and clerks to have one or two years of college. Many community and junior colleges offer courses in this field. Some offer programs that combine classroom study with on-the-job experience. Students who complete such programs earn as associate degree or a certificate of completion.

Traffic agents and clerks may be required to be licensed or certified. Requirements vary depending on the state and the employer.

Earnings

The job outlook for these workers is good through the early 1990s. Openings will continue to occur as new businesses are developed. Traffic agents and clerks will retire or change jobs. This will create more job openings. However, automation of this job with computers may somewhat slow the need for new workers.

Beginning salaries for traffic agents and clerks averaged about $16,000 in the early 1990s. Starting salaries depend on the particular field of traffic entered. They also depend on the job seeker's level of education and amount of related work experience.

Ways of getting more information

For more information abut a career as a traffic agent or traffic clerk write to:

▶ National Freight Transportation Association
   PO Box 21856
   Roanoke, VA 24018

▶ The responsibility of registering each package that is to be shipped is the role of the traffic agent.

Travel Agents

Other Articles to Look At:

▶ **Car-Rental Agents**
▶ **Hotel Clerks**
▶ **Reservation and Transportation Ticket Agents**
▶ **Secretaries**
▶ **Tour Guides**

What travel agents do

Travel agents help people plan vacations and business trips by providing information about transportation, hotels or motels, and sightseeing opportunities. Agents make tour reservations, prepare tickets, and advise people on passport and visa requirements. Although there is the possibility of traveling to far-away places, a travel agents usually work in offices making detailed travel arrangements and then making sure those arrangements are correct.

A travel agent must be part salesperson, part travel consultant, and part bookkeeper. Agents must first discuss the travel needs of a customer (such as where and when a person wants to travel, how much money they can afford to spend, and how long they can stay away) and then present the client with a travel plan that meets those needs. The agent may suggest a package tour or arrange for the person to stay in a number of places over a specified period of time.

Travel agents consult a variety of sources to get the desired arrival and departure times, find the most reasonably priced airplane fares, and arrange hotel rooms or make other reservations. Most agents use computers to discover flight schedules and the various prices of hotel and motel accommodations. Agents often use their own experiences when making reservations.

For inexperienced travelers, the travel agent may review what to bring on a trip and what to expect once travelers reach their destination. For example, an agent may provide travelers with a guide book and explain the best ways to change money into a foreign currency.

Agents may also give slide presentations or lectures to interested groups or place advertisements in newspapers in order to promote their services.

Education and training

Travel agents should have a well-rounded education. Good communications skills, including the ability to write and speak clearly, are important. In addition, knowledge of one or more foreign languages (Spanish, French, and so on) will be of help when dealing with travelers or other people from a foreign country. Travel agents must have a solid background in world geography and must keep up-to-date on world events so that questions about upcoming events (such as the Olympics) can be anticipated and areas experiencing conflict (such as countries having serious political problems) can be avoided. As in many other professions, computer skills are becoming increasingly important—agents are constantly using computers to make travel reservations.

Students interested in becoming a travel agent should take classes in geography, English, and history, as well as business-related courses, such as typing and mathematics. Many employers prefer to hire college graduates, although a person with a high-school diploma may also find success. There are also special training programs for travel agents and most travel agencies give on-the-job training to new employees.

Earnings

With individuals and families increasingly taking long vacations and weekend trips the whole year round, job opportunities for travel agents are expected to grow rapidly during the early 1990s. Because many people consider this an exciting profession, there may be a good deal of competition for these positions.

Salaries for travel agents range between $12,000 and $24,000 a year, depending on experience and the size of the company. Travel agents may be paid a regular salary, paid entirely on a commission basis (based on how many people use their services), or receive a salary plus a commission. An advantage of working as a travel agent is that when agents themselves take a trip, they get substantially reduced prices on airplane tickets and hotel rates. Sometimes, an agent may get a free (or almost free) trip for promotional purposes.

Ways of getting more information

A good way to find out about being a travel agent is to get a part-time or summer job in

▶ A travel agent explains train schedules to a couple planning a trip abroad.

a travel agency. Conversations with travel agents as well as reading travel writings are also good ways of learning more about this career.

In addition, write to the following and ask for information about being a travel agent:

▶ American Society of Travel Agents
  1101 King Street
  Alexandria, VA 22314

▶ Institute of Certified Travel Agents
  148 Linden Street
  Wellesley, MA 02181

Truck Drivers

Other Articles to Look At:

▶ **Bus Drivers**
▶ **Industrial Truck Drivers**
▶ **Route Drivers**
▶ **Taxi Drivers**

What truck drivers do

Truck drivers can be divided into two categories. *Local truck drivers* are sometimes called *short haulers*. These drivers operate vehicles to transport materials, merchandise, equipment or people within a limited area. They may load and unload their trucks by hand, or they may use a cable wince or hoist. Short haulers may be expected to make minor repairs to their vehicles and otherwise keep them in good working order.

Over-the-road truck drivers are called *long haulers*. They are also known as *trailer-truck drivers*. They transport goods over long distances in gasoline or diesel-powered tractor-trailer. They frequently drive at night.

Local truck drivers must be skilled drivers. They have to maneuver their trucks through congested city traffic. They must be able to fit into tight parking spaces, drive through narrow alleys, and back up to platforms.

Drivers of light trucks (under three tons) pick up and deliver light loads. They load and unload their own vehicles. Local truck drivers usually do not make deliveries along established routes. Instead, they deliver their ma-terials to whichever addresses are listed on the freight bills. Drivers must check these freight bills carefully to be sure they are delivering the correct merchandise to the right people. They must turn in daily records of the deliveries they have made.

Local drivers of heavy trucks (over three tons) generally have a helper who assists with the loading and unloading of the truck. Drivers of moving vans usually have a crew of helpers. Otherwise, their duties are similar to those of light truck drivers. Some heavy truck drivers operate special vehicles. These include dump trucks, oil and gasoline truck's, and cement-mixing trucks.

Over-the-road drivers must also be highly skilled at their work. They must be able to back up their huge trailers to loading docks. These drivers must inspect their trucks before and after long trips and keep a daily log.

Two types of employers hire over-the-road drivers. Private carriers include chain food stores and large manufacturing plants that pick up and deliver their own goods. For-hire carriers are trucking firms that serve both the general public (common carriers) and specific companies (contract carriers). Most over-the-road drivers are employed by common carriers. Drivers who work for common carriers and contract carriers often own or lease their trucks.

Education and training

A high-school education is desirable for persons wanting to become truck drivers. Driv-

▶ Using a citizen's band radio, a truck driver radios to other drivers to find out about road and traffic conditions.

er's education courses and auto shop classes are especially helpful.

Most trucking companies prefer to hire drivers who are at least twenty-one and preferably twenty-five years old. Drivers should have as much driving experience as possible. Over-the-road drivers must meet standards set by the Interstate Commerce Commission. They must have at lease one year of driving experience (automobile driving is included) and have good driving records. In addition, all truck drivers must have a commercial driver's license.

Earnings

The need for truck drivers is expected to increase about as fast as average in the early 1990s. Competition will be strong as many people are attracted to this work by its high salaries.

In the early 1990s, salaries for local truck drivers averaged $12.00 an hour and $14.00 an hour for all drivers. Long distance drivers earned about $30,000 per year in the early 1990s. Some earn more than $50,000.

Ways of getting more information

For more information write to:

▶ American Trucking Association
2200 Mill Road
Alexandria, VA 22314

Typesetters

Other Articles to Look At:

▶ **Bindery Workers**
▶ **Lithographic Workers**
▶ **Photoengravers**
▶ **Photographic Equipment Technicians**
▶ **Printing Press Operators**
▶ **Typists**

What typesetters do

Typesetters set the type and prepare the printing plates that are needed to print newspapers, books, magazines, advertisements, business forms, and calendars. Anything that is printed in mass form must first pass through the hands of the typesetter before it goes on to the printing press.

Typesetters first select the type style and size according to instructions for the job to be done. They then arranges, or sets, the type in correct order and in the proper place on the page, along with any necessary breaks or photoengravings (photos). Type can be set by hand or on the keyboard of a linotype or monotype machine, but most typesetters today use the electronic keyboard of a computerized phototypesetting machine.

After the type has been properly set, a sample of the printed material is made. This sample, called a "proof," is carefully examined for mistakes so that the typesetter can correct them before final copies are printed.

Typesetters must be careful, accurate workers with a thorough understanding of the mechanical or electronic machines they use. They need a good command of the English language and should be proficient in spelling, grammar, and arithmetic.

Education and training

A high-school education is usually a requirement for becoming a typesetter, with courses in printing and typewriting being especially good preparation. Most typesetters learn their trade as helpers or apprentices in the composing room. Apprenticeships usually take from four to six years, depending on the individual's previous experience or education. Helpers, who usually work in nonunion small shops, pick up their skills in the course of their work. Unlike in apprenticeship programs, employers aren't required to give helpers definitely planned and scheduled instruction.

There are many different occupations in the printing field, so advancement opportunities are plentiful for ambitious workers. One common ambition of typesetters and printers is to have shops of their own, and many of the printing establishments in this country are one-person shops operated by their owners.

Earnings

Although many jobs are opening up for keyboard operators in computerized phototypesetting, the employment outlook for most

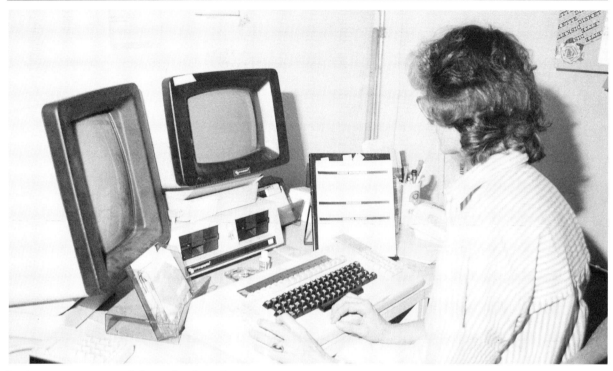

▶ A typesetter enters information into the computer with printing codes to set type size and style.

composing room occupations isn't promising. Automation has replaced many workers, and it will be the workers with the greatest technical knowledge and abilities who find the best jobs of the future.

In the early 1990s, experienced union typesetters made an average annual salary of about $22,880.

Ways of getting more information

Libraries have many books and magazines on the history and development of the printing industry. For a firsthand look at what typesetters do, try to arrange a visit to a newspaper or other commercial printing establishment.

For more information write to:

▶ Book Manufacturers Institute
111 Prospect
Stamford, CT 06901

▶ Graphic Arts Technical Foundation
4615 Forbes Avenue
Pittsburgh, PA 15213

▶ Printing Industries of America
1730 North Lynn Street
Arlington, VA 22209

▶ Printing, Publishing, and Media
Workers Sector of CWA
1925 K Street, NW
Washington, DC 20006

▶ Typographers International Association
2262 Hall Place, NW
Washington, DC 20007

Typists

Other Articles to Look At:

► **Computer Operating Personnel**
► **Legal Assistants**
► **Medical Record Administrators**
► **Receptionists**
► **Secretaries and Stenographers**

What typists do

Typewriters, word processors, and other office machines are important parts of any work place. *Typists* use these machines to change handwritten material into clean, easy-to-read typewritten copies, typists work on reports, letters. forms, charts, and many other projects for all types of businesses and services. *Word-processing operators* use computers that store material electronically instead of printing it directly on paper. Word processors are quickly replacing typewriters in many offices even though both machines are still in wide use.

Some typists only duty is to type. Others spend most of their time typing but have clerical jobs, such as filing, answering the phone, and running the copy machine, which they do, too. Typists may work in small offices, or they may be part of a typing pool of a hundred workers or more workers. They usually work in modern, well-lighted and pleasant surroundings.

Among the different job categories ln this field are: *clerk typists*, who type reports, bills, and forms. Other workers type from recorded tapes instead of written or typed copy. These typists are called *word processing operators*. The keyboard of a word-processor is much like that of a typewriter except the numbers and letters show up as letter and numbers on a video display terminal (VDT). These typists can edit, change, and insert materials just by pressing keys, which make the errors disappear. When work-processing operators have finished typing a document, it is automatically sent to a dot-matrix or laser printer that produces a document that looks typewritten.

Education and training

Most typists should have a high-school diploma and be able to type neatly, correctly, and quickly. Typists should have a good knowledge of spelling, grammar, and punctuation. Typing skills are taught in high schools, colleges, business schools, and home-study courses. In addition, computer and word-processing classes are taught at most community colleges and business schools.

For those who have not had word-processing training in school, many employers profile training to new employees. The makers of word-processing equipment also offer classes to introduce the basics of operating their equipment. In general, it takes three to six months of hands-on experience to become a good word-processing operator.

▶ With the information to be typed on a board beside her, a typist copies the information onto another page.

Earnings

About one million people were employed as typists during the early 1990s. Most worked in business, but many others worked in education, medicine, and government. The demand for typists, especially those skilled in work-processing, will be high for many years to come.

The average pay for beginning typists was about $13,500 per year, with experienced workers earning an average of $17,500. The top in the field earn more than $24,000 per year.

Ways of getting more information

A good way to get experience in this field is through a high-school work/study program. Students in these programs work part-time for local businesses and go to school part-time.

For additional information write to the following;

▶ The Association of Independent
Colleges and Schools
One Dupont Circle, Suite 350
Washington, DC 20036

▶ Association of Information Systems
Professionals
104 Wilmot Road
Deerfield, IL 60015

▶ Professional Secretaries International
801 East Armour Boulevard
Kansas City, MO 64111

Umpires

Other Articles to Look At:

▶ **Judges**
▶ **Personnel and Labor Relations Specialists**
▶ **Recreation Workers**
▶ **Sports Coaches**
▶ **Sports Instructors**

What umpires do

Umpires and other sports officials enforce the rules and regulations of a particular sport and make decisions on disputed matters during a sporting contest. The term "umpire" is usually used to refer to those who officiate at baseball games; basketball, football, soccer, and the other sports often use the term *referee* or *linesmen* for these officials. Although some umpires are involved with professional baseball, the vast majority work for minor league and amateur teams.

An umpire must often start work well before a game begins. Umpires inspect the playing field before the game to make sure it is in good condition and check the baseballs and bats to see that they are regulation size and weight.

During the game, umpires must carefully watch the action. There are usually four umpires at a professional baseball game; amateur contests may have one or two umpires. Each umpire has specific responsibilities. The plate umpire calls balls and strikes. This requires careful attention and quick decisions after the pitcher throws the ball. When the ball is hit, the umpires watch the ball to see if it lands in fair or foul territory and to see if a fielder catches the ball or the ball falls safely into play. Umpires must be careful not to interfere with play and not to make decisions too quickly because an outfielder may drop a ball at the last second or a fielder may illegally block a player from running around the bases.

Sometimes umpires must make important decisions that anger and upset some of the players and fans. Umpires may get into arguments with managers and players, but more often than not, umpires make their decisions without much controversy.

Umpires must travel a great deal. Professional umpires travel around the country and rarely spend more than a day or two at home during the season. Amateur umpires work closer to home, but they too travel a great deal and work evenings and weekends.

Education and training

Umpires and other sports officials should have a comprehensive understanding of a sport and its rules. They also need good judgment, integrity, and the ability to make quick, accurate decisions. Umpires should also have excellent eyesight (with or without correction) and be in good physical condition.

Umpires may be called on to make important decisions in a matter of seconds. They must have confidence in their ability to make such decisions and should be able to handle the pressure of having people disagree with them (sometimes rather strongly).

There are no specific educational requirements. Umpires at the amateur level are often former players or coaches who understand the game and know the rules. These umpires may attend a one-day clinic several times a year to review the rules and discuss umpiring techniques. Those who want to umpire on the professional level should have at least several years of minor league umpiring experience and complete a two-month training program at a school for umpires. These programs feature a comprehensive review of the rules and regulations. Many of the classes are taught by professional umpires.

Earnings

There are only limited opportunities to work as an umpire, especially at the professional level. There are fewer than 100 major league umpires, and minor league opportunities are also fairly rare.

Earnings vary greatly, depending on at which level an umpire is employed. Major league umpires earn about $75,000 per year, with bonuses for working championship games such as the World Series. Minor league umpires earn about $1,200 a month, but they normally work only during the summer months. Other umpires may earn $15 to $20 per game.

Ways of getting more information

A good way to find out if you would enjoy being an umpire is to officiate at a summer

▶ An umpire watches a race to the plate to determine if the runner made it there first.

camp or work for a Little League or similar organization. It might also be possible to talk with an umpire and in that way learn more about the profession.

In addition, write to the following organizations and ask for information about being an umpire:

▶ Major League Umpires Association
One Logan Square, Suite 1004
Philadelphia, PA 19103

▶ National Association of Leagues, Umpires and Scorers
PO Box 1420
Wichita, KS 67201

Underwriters

Other Articles to Look At:

▶ **Actuaries**
▶ **Bank Officers and Managers**
▶ **Life Insurance Agents and Brokers**
▶ **Insurance Policy Processing Occupations**
▶ **Bank Clerks**

What underwriters do

Underwriters decide whether or not an insurance company should agree to insure someone and how much that person will have to pay for insurance.

People want insurance to protect themselves against serious accidents or big losses. For example, if a family's house burns down, they may not be able to afford to buy another one. To protect themselves in case this happens, they apply for fire insurance. This means that the family pays the insurance company a small amount of money every month. Then if the house does burn down, the insurance company pays the family an amount of money to help them buy a new one. In other words, the insurance company will cover the risk of fire for that family.

The insurance company can afford to cover one family's loss because it receives money every month from many families who do not lose their houses. Insurance companies have to make sure that they do not cover risks that would be financially unsound.

It is the underwriter's job to make sure that the insurance company does not take bad risks. For example, if someone wants fire insurance on a building with bad wiring or an unsafe furnace, the underwriter may decide that the risk of fire in this building is too great. Then the underwriter can either refuse to insure the building; agree to insure it after repairs are made; or charge a higher monthly payment for insurance.

Underwriters work in quiet offices. They receive applications from people who want insurance for all kinds of things. Life insurance will pay if the insured person dies; disability insurance will pay insured workers who have accidents or illnesses that prevent them from working. Property insurance covers damage or loss of almost any kind of property— houses, boats, jewelry, cars, bridges, airplanes, or paintings.

Underwriters must look at the information in each application carefully. They have to analyze what kinds of risks are involved. Then they study statistics on how likely these risks are to occur. Underwriters make decisions based on many technical details. They must be able to weigh all the facts and take responsibility for their decisions. Insurance companies depend on the good judgment of their underwriters.

Education and training

Most insurance companies look for college graduates to fill underwriting jobs. The bach-

▶ An underwriter prepares a report on the insurance policy of a prospective client.

elor's degree may be in any field, although a degree in business may be especially helpful. Smaller companies may hire high-school graduates as clerks and then train them. Most insurance companies want their underwriters to keep up with new developments in the field by taking part-time classes.

Earnings

As the insurance business expands in the 1990s, there will be many new positions for underwriters.

An average salary for an underwriter is about $21,500 a year. Senior underwriters earn up to $27,000. Those who supervise other underwriters average $31,000 a year; those who manage an entire department earn up to $37,000.

Ways of getting more information

Talking with an insurance agent will give you an idea of how insurance companies work and what different jobs are available.

For more information write to:

▶ American Council of Life Insurance
  1001 Pennsylania Avenue, NW
  Washington, DC 20004

▶ Insurance Information Institute
  110 William Street
  New York, NY 10038

▶ The National Association of
  Independent Insurers
  Public Relations Department
  2600 River Road
  Des Plaines, IL 60618

Ushers

Other Articles to Look At:

▶ **Counter and Retail Clerks**
▶ **Door-to-Door Sales Workers**
▶ **Gaming Occupations**
▶ **Hotel Clerks**
▶ **Motion Picture Theater Workers**
▶ **Tour Guides**

What ushers do

Crowd control is an important consideration at any public event. Whether that event is a football game attended by 60,000 fans in a huge stadium or a piano recital for sixty music enthusiasts in a small hall, someone must help people find their seats, maintain order, and keep people calm in the even of a crisis. These duties are performed at public events by *ushers.*

Ushers work everywhere that crowds gather. They work at movie houses, concert halls, sports stadiums, circuses, music festivals, and other public events. Their main job is to seat patrons. However, depending on the nature of the event, ushers perform many other duties as well.

For example, at sporting events, ushers must maintain order. Sports fans can become quite unruly, especially if the home team is losing or the umpires or referees are making unpopular decisions. Ushers help to calm the fans. Should a fight occur, ushers must either break up the fight and escort the fighters out of the stadium or call for security guards. Ushers must also prevent fans from taking seats other than those they paid for.

At movie theaters, ushers erect barriers to keep moviegoers in line, take tickets, and direct patrons to refreshment counters and restrooms. After the movie has started and the theater is darkened, ushers may escort late arrivals to empty seats. Ushers must also field complaints from patrons about poor sound or picture quality and ask people not to talk during the film. Should someone lose a wallet or a purse, the usher, using a small flashlight, helps that person find the missing article. At the end of the movie, ushers direct people out of the theater and may be responsible for cleaning the theater before the next show.

At theaters where live stage shows are presented, seats are usually reserved. Ushers must read the seat assignments on tickets and escort theatergoers to the proper seats. During the performance, ushers must seat any late arrivals as quickly and quietly as possible.

Should a crisis occur, such as a fire in a theater, ushers must act quickly and calmly to get people out of the theater using emergency exit doors.

Some ushers work directly for the stadium, theater, or concert hall where events are held. Other ushers, however, work for companies that specialize in providing ushers for public gatherings. These ushers may work basketball game one night, a concert the next night, and a circus the third night.

▶ An usher directs ticketholders to their seats at a football game.

Education and training
There are no formal educational requirements for ushers. Most employers train their own ushers. This training period us usually brief.

Earnings
The need for ushers in the early 1990s will be strong. Workers in the field often leave to take higher paying work and so there is a continual need to replace these people.

Ushers are usually paid a minimum wage. Some ushers earn as little as $60 a week or as much as $150. Assistant or head ushers can earn $5.00 to $6.00 an hour.

Ways of getting more information
For more information about a career as an usher, contact:

▶ Services Employees International Union
  1313 L Street, NW
  Washington, DC 20005

Vending-Machine Mechanics

Other Articles to Look At:

▶ **Appliance Repairers**
▶ **Electromechanical Technicians**
▶ **Industrial Machinery Mechanics**
▶ **Machinists**
▶ **Office-Machine Servicers**

What vending-machine mechanics do

Vending machines, coin-operated machines that dispense items such as soft drinks, soup, sandwiches, and candy, can be found in stores, schools, and many other locations. *Vending-machine mechanics* install these machines and keep them in good operating condition. They test new machines to make sure they are working properly, check and clean these machines on a regular basis, and make any necessary repairs.

Before new machines are installed, mechanics make sure they are in good working order. Most vending machines have complicated electrical connections that require close inspection. A beverage dispenser, for example, has ice-making and refrigerator systems for cold drinks or heating units for coffee and other hot drinks. Mechanics must make sure that the machine mixes the drinks properly, that the dispenser does not overfill or underfill the cups, and that the change-making system works. When installing the machines, mechanics connect the machines to electrical and water sources. Then they fill the machines with ingredients or products and retest the machines for proper operations.

When a machine breaks down, mechanics must figure out the cause of the problem. Loose electrical wires, coin-operation troubles, and beverage leaks are relatively easy to spot; more difficult problems might require the use of a testing device to find defective parts. Mechanics often repair or replace broken parts at the site, but for complicated problems they might replace the machine and bring the broken machine to the repair shop.

A major part of the mechanics' job is preventative maintenance. They check the machines regularly to prevent problems before they occur. For example, they put grease on mechanical parts and clean electrical connections to keep the machines performing properly. This is especially important with machines that are used a great deal (as many of them are).

Mechanics also have some clerical responsibilities, such as writing reports, preparing cost estimates, and ordering parts. They also stock the machines with merchandise, collect the money, make sure the machines have enough coins to make change, and keep daily sales records.

Education and training

Vending-machine mechanics should have a strong interest in mechanical subjects and be able to work with their hands. They need to be skillful in using hammers, screwdrivers, and other handtools and power tools, such as saws and drills. Because mechanics handle large amounts of cash, they should be trustworthy. A pleasant personality is important so that mechanics can deal effectively with the many different types of people in the businesses and other locations where the machines are located.

Most mechanics learn their skills on the job by working alongside experienced mechanics for several weeks or months. New workers usually start by doing simple tasks such as putting products into a machine, and gradually learn how to repair and replace broken equipment. Although most employers prefer to hire high-school graduates, a degree is not always necessary.

A three-year apprenticeship program is offered by the National Automatic Merchandising Association to help employers train some workers. The program provides several weeks of classroom training each year in subjects such as basic electricity, blueprint reading, customer relations, and safety.

▶ With the cup dispenser pulled out, a vending-machine mechanic refills the supplies in the machine.

Earnings

Although more and more establishments are installing vending machines, future job opportunities will be somewhat limited. This is because newer machines break down less often and therefore require less maintenance. Despite limited job opportunities, skilled mechanics should continue to find employment.

The average salary is between $16,000 and $20,000 per year, although some highly skilled mechanics can earn more than $25,000 annually.

Ways of getting more information

To find out more about vending-machine mechanics take a course in machine repair or get a part-time job as a mechanic's helper.

In addition, write to the following organization and ask for information about being a vending-machine mechanic:

▶ National Automatic Merchandising Association
  20 North Wacker Drive
  Chicago, IL 60606

Veterinarians

Other Articles to Look At:

▶ **Agricultural Engineers**
▶ **Animal Health Technicians**
▶ **Animal Production Technicians**

What veterinarians do

Veterinarians treat diseased and injured animals and give advice on how to care for and breed healthy animals. Veterinarians treat not only dogs, cats, and other small pets, but may also work with farm or zoo animals. Still others do research to find causes and cures of diseases.

Most small-animal doctors work in their offices. They do surgery, treat minor illnesses, and board sick and healthy animals who need a temporary place to stay. Sometimes they provide emergency house calls, but most try to keep normal business hours. A few doctors may work as many as sixty hours a week if an emergency health problem exists.

In small towns or in the country, veterinarians may travel long distances to treat animals. Some large cattle ranches or horse farms keep veterinarians on their staff. Most zoos also employ a full-time veterinarian to handle the health care, feeding, and treatment of the entire animal collection.

Many veterinarians work as inspectors in meat packing and chicken processing companies. They examine the meat for signs of disease. A small number of veterinarians also teach in schools of veterinary medicine.

Education and training

To set up private practice as a veterinarian, a person must have a degree in doctor of veterinary medicine (D.V.M.) and pass an examination by a state licensing board. Usually a degree can be achieved seven or eight years after graduation from high school. Most accredited schools of veterinary medicine in the United States offer four-year programs. But some require five years to complete the degree. And most require that a student complete at least two years of general college courses before being admitted to the veterinarian program.

Many preveterinary students obtain a bachelor's degree from a four-year college before applying for admission to the D.V.M. degree program. Because of limited facilities, less than half of the students applying to schools of veterinary medicine are admitted. Good grades in high school and preveterinary college are essential.

Upon completion of a D.V.M. degree, students are required to pass an examination from the state board of licensing.

Earnings

There will always be a demand for veterinarians, although competition for jobs may be stiff. Veterinarians with the best training will have the most opportunity for advancement.

Generally, veterinarians just starting out in private practice can expect to make between $18,000 and $21,000 a year. Those in more established careers make $46,000 or more per year. Those who work for the federal government will make slightly less.

Ways of getting more information

Visiting with local veterinarians in their office, at a farm, a ranch, a zoo, or at college or university is an excellent way to learn more about the day-to-day work of veterinarians.

In school, study biology and animal-related sciences. Joining a 4-H Club and participating in projects involving the care of animals is also valuable. Many veterinarians accept volunteers to help with feeding the animals and cleaning their cages. Part-time or summer work may also be available in veterinary offices, in zoos, or on farms.

For more information write to the following sources:

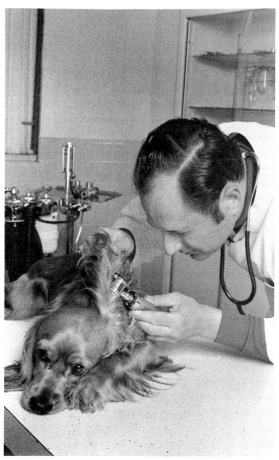

▶ A veterianarian examines the ear on a sick dog.

▶ American Veterinary Medical Association
930 North Meacham Road
Schaumburg, IL 60196

▶ U.S. Department of Agriculture
Animal and Plant Health Inspection Service
Veterinary Services, Training/ Information Management Staff
Room 853, Federal Building
Hyattsville, MD 20782

▶ U.S. Department of Agriculture
Food Safety and Inspection Service, Personnel Division
Butler Square West, 4th Floor
100 North 6th Street
Minneapolis, MN 55403

Video Technicians

Other Articles to Look At:

▶ **Audio-Control Technicians**
▶ **Cable-Television Technicians**
▶ **Communications Equipment Mechanics**
▶ **Radio and Television Program Directors**
▶ **Sound-Recording Technicians**
▶ **Studio Technicians**

What video technicians do

Video technicians usually work in television stations. They are involved in several different aspects of broadcasting and videotaping television programs. Technicians who are mostly involved with broadcasting programs are often called *video-control technicians*. Those who are mostly involved with taping programs are often called *videotape-recording technicians*.

Video-control technicians work under the direction of the television program director. They operate equipment that controls the picture that is sent to the transmitter for broadcast. During a studio production, several cameras record the show, and the picture from each camera is displayed in the studio control room. The director indicates which camera's picture should be used, and the technician switches that picture to the transmitter or videotape machine. Video-control

technicians also control the quality of the picture by operating switches that adjust color balance, brightness, framing, vertical hold, and contrast.

Some programs require that video-control technicians combine pictures coming from different sources. They may mix together scenes being performed in different studios, blend live with taped segments, or switch between studio and on-the-scene transmissions. The broadcasting of instant replays, which are very common in live sports events, is another responsibility of video-control technicians.

In addition, video-control technicians monitor programs that are on the air to make sure that their picture quality is good. They also keep a daily record of all programs that are sent to the transmitter.

Videotape-recording technicians use special cameras and tape-recording equipment to videotape live shows. They also copy segments from one videotape to another in order to combine several scenes into a finished program. They sometimes create special effects using the recording and rerecording equipment.

Videotape-recording technicians prepare for a show by checking that their equipment is in working order and making sure that they understand what they are to record and how they are to record it. During the show they monitor sound and picture quality and make adjustments as necessary.

Videotape-recording technicians also do routine maintenance on their equipment and sometimes do minor repairs.

Education and training

While in high school, students interested in this career should take courses in mathematics, science (especially courses that include physics), and English. They should also try to take radio and television broadcasting or electronics courses.

After high school, they need to receive further training in television technology at a technical institute or a junior or community college that offers a two-year course of study in television broadcasting and electronics.

Earnings

The number of people employed as video technicians is expected to increase in early 1990s. However, there will be strong competition for jobs in big cities, where the number of applicants will probably exceed the number of jobs available. Opportunities will probably be much better in small cities.

Video technicians earn salaries that average about $22,000 a year. Beginning technicians usually earn less than this amount. Very experienced technicians can earn as much as $50,000 a year or more. Technicians working in cities make more than those in rural areas. Technicians working for educational television stations usually earn less than those working for commercial stations.

Ways of getting more information

A good way to learn more about this career is through a visit to a local television station. Students can also explore this field by belonging to a high-school club or other organization that is involved with electronics or radio and television broadcasting.

In addition, students can write for more information from the following organizations:

▶ A video technician cuts and edits videotape on a splicing machine.

▶ National Association Broadcast Employees and Technicians
7101 Wisconsin Avenue, Suite 800
Bethesda, MD 20814

▶ National Association of Broadcasters Employment Clearinghouse
1771 N Street, NW
Washington, DC 20036

▶ National Cable Television Association
1724 Massachusetts Avenue, NW
Washington, DC 20036

Waiters and Waitresses

Other Articles to Look At:

▶ **Bakers**
▶ **Bartenders**
▶ **Cooks and Chefs**
▶ **Flight Attendants**
▶ **Food Service Workers**
▶ **Restaurant Managers**

What waiters and waitresses do

Waiters and waitresses are part of the food service industry. Their primary function is to serve food and beverages to customers in restaurants and other food establishments. In addition to this task, waiters and waitresses also take customers' orders, make out bills, and collect money.

Informal waiters and waitresses work in small, casual food establishments. These include diners, fast food restaurants, grills, cafeterias, and sandwich shops. In addition to their regular duties, they may also be required to clear and clean tables and counters. As part of servicing their customers, they may prepare salads and beverages, dish out prepared foods such as soups and stews, replenish supplies, and set up tables for future customers. In some establishments, waiters and waitresses are also expected to clean equipment, sweep and mop floors, and carry out trash.

Large restaurants employ *formal waiters and waitresses,* many of whom perform spe-

cific tasks. For example, there is often a *headwaiter* or *headwaitress* who greets arriving customers, checks on their reservations, and escorts them to their tables. These employees are sometimes called *captains.* The waiter or waitress who takes the diners' orders may make suggestions about which dishes are especially appetizing. They may also recite a list of specials—dishes that the chef has prepared for that evening and that do not appear on the menu.

Some waiters and waitresses specialize in dispensing alcoholic and nonalcoholic beverages. These employees are called *bartenders.* Many formal restaurants also employ waiters and waitresses whose sole responsibility is to serve wine. These *wine stewards* present a list of available wines to the diners and may make suggestions about which wines would be appropriate with the food the diners have ordered. The wine steward then brings the diner's selection to the table, opens the bottle, and pours the wine. Periodically throughout the meal, the wine steward will return to refill the diners' glasses.

Waiters and waitresses do not work just in restaurants. Some work in bars, in hotel dining rooms, and in the dining cars of trains. In large hotels, room service waiters and waitresses bring food from the hotel's kitchen to the rooms of the hotel guests.

Education and training

Although there are no formal educational requirements to become waiters and wait-

▶ A waitress takes a family's order for dinner and then brings the food to the table.

resses, persons interested in such a career are advised to earn a high-school diploma. Most restaurants like to train their own waiters and waitresses.

Many technical and vocational schools offer training programs for waiters and waitresses along with full programs in food service management. Persons with such training will have an easier time being hired than those without it.

Earnings

Job opportunities for waiters and waitresses are expected to be plentiful in the early 1990s.

Waiters and waitresses are usually paid the minimum wage by their employers. These workers also receive tips from their custom-ers. The tip is usually fifteen to twenty percent of the total bill.

In the early 1990s, waiters and waitresses earned an average of $9,400 a year, excluding tips. Half of these workers earned between $6,000 and $12,000 a year. One-tenth earned more than $15,500 per year.

Ways of getting more information
For more information write to:

▶ National Institute for the Food Service Industry
250 South Wacker Drive
Chicago, IL 60606

Watch Repairers

Other Articles to Look At:

▶ **Assemblers**
▶ **Electromechanical Technicians**
▶ **Instrument Repairers**
▶ **Jewelers and Jewelry Repairers**
▶ **Locksmiths**
▶ **Mechanical Technicians**

What watch repairers do

Watch repairers repair, adjust, clean, and regulate watches, clocks, and other kinds of timepieces. They may work at home or in department stores, shopping centers, jewelry stores, or repair shops.

Watches are complex machines with many small parts, and to repair one requires precision and delicacy. The first skill a watch repairer needs is the ability to determine exactly what is wrong with the watch. Asking the customer about the past history and current problem gives some information; visually observing and checking the winding stem may give other clues. The next step is to open the case and remove the dial so the mechanism itself can be examined using a magnifying glass, or loupe.

Watch repairers check for such defects as broken parts, rusting springs, or misalignment of parts. They clean, oil, repair, replace, and rebuild parts as necessary before reassembling the watch so that everything fits together properly. They use a variety of tools to help them, from simple pliers and tweezers to sophisticated electronic timing devices. Everything they do requires great patience and a delicate touch, and experienced and skilled repairers are always in demand.

Some watch repairers do jewelry repair work and sell items like clocks, watches, jewelry, china, and silverware. This is especially true if they are self-employed or work in a retail store.

Education and training

The best way to become a watch repairer is to complete the training offered by an established watch repair school. This training takes one to three years to complete, and the course of study includes taking apart and putting together watches, cleaning and oiling the working mechanisms, and repairing and replacing parts in various kinds of timepieces. Those persons interested in going into business for themselves would also benefit from basic business, advertising, and accounting courses, and from training in engraving, jewel repair, and stone setting.

Although a high-school diploma is not necessarily required to become a successful watch repairer, those with one will find greater ease in advancement and in business dealings.

Earnings

Though skilled watch repairers will always be in demand, general job opportunities in this

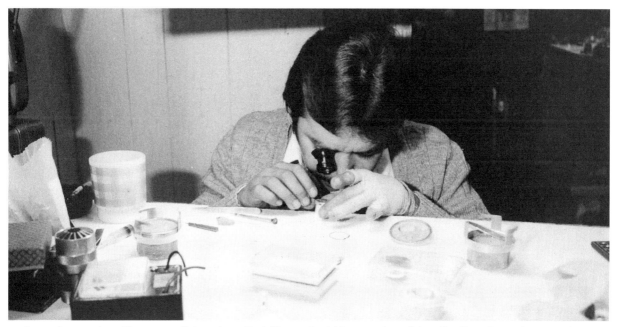

▶ A repairer works with a magnifying glass that fits against his eye when fixing the tiny pieces in a watch.

field will be below average through the next decade. More and more people are buying inexpensive watches these days, and it is often cheaper and easier to replace a broken watch than it is to fix it. However, the person who owns a good watch will usually continue to have it repaired, and ambitious workers who save enough money can always hope to open their own repair shop or retail watch and jewelry store.

In the early 1990s, beginning watch repairers earned anywhere from $9,100 to $14,600 a year. Experienced workers earned from $15,600 to more than $26,000, and supervisors and service managers in large repair shops earned considerably more. Self-employed watchmakers earned between $15,000 and $23,000 a year, while those who sold jewelry, china, and other items in addition to watches could earn up to $40,000 a year, or even more.

Ways of getting more information

Libraries have books on the subject of watchmaking and repairing; for a closer look, visit a local watchmaker and observe him or her at work. Any hobbies that call for careful handwork could serve as useful preparation as well.

For more information write to:

▶ American Watchmakers Institute
3700 Harrison Avenue
Cincinnati, OH 45211

▶ Jewelers of America
1271 Avenue of the Americas
New York, NY 10020

▶ Service Employees International Union
1313 L Street, NW
Washington, DC 20005

Water and Wastewater Treatment-Plant Operators

Other Articles to Look At:

▶ **Electricians**
▶ **Health and Regulatory Inspectors**
▶ **Chemical Technicians**
▶ **Pollution-Control Technicians**
▶ **Industrial Machinery Mechanics**

What water and wastewater treatment-plant operators do

water and wastewater treatment-plant operators run the plants that take harmful chemicals and wastes out of water. They make sure the water is safe to use again. They are also called *sewage plant operators.*

Water carrying waste materials flows through sewer pipes to a sewage treatment plant. The water contains human waste that could spread disease. It also contains industrial waste—chemicals, such as mercury and lead—that are poisonous. At the treatment plant, this wastewater, or sewage, goes through different cleaning processes until all the dangerous materials are removed.

The plant operators control how fast wastewater flows into the plant. During floods, they have to make emergency adjustments. As the sewage flows from one processing pool to another, the plant operators make sure all the equipment is working properly. If necessary, they make minor repairs.

They take samples of the wastewater at different stages to check its waste content. They also perform laboratory tests on the waste and keep a record of plant operations. Because clean water is absolutely necessary for any community, the federal government requires the water coming from treatment plants to meet standards of cleanliness. As government standards become stricter, the process of treating wastewater becomes more complicated. Plant operators must be able to understand different processes and operate complicated machinery.

Wastewater treatment plants must keep running night and day, so the operators work in shifts around the clock. During emergencies, they may have to work extra hours. The constant need for wastewater treatment makes plant operators jobs very secure.

Operators work both indoors and outdoor checking and repairing noisy equipment.

Most operators are employed by local governments; some work for the federal government or utility companies. In larger treatment plants, the operator will supervise attendants who perform with routine tasks. In small plants, one operator may be responsible for running the plant.

Education and training

Most employers prefer to hire high-school graduates for plant operator jobs. High-school courses in mathematics and machine shop will be useful. Beyond high school, there are two-year programs in wastewater technology; however, beginning sewage plant operators usually learn on the job. They begin as trainees working with an experienced operator.

Some plants may offer a training program. State water pollution control agencies offer courses to keep operators up-to-date and to expand their knowledge of water treatment processes.

In large cities, the operator jobs may require applicants to take a civil service exam. In most states, an operator who supervises a plant must be certified. To earn certification, operators must pass an exam.

Earnings

The demand for wastewater treatment-plant operators will grow only slightly in the 1990s. There will be more jobs in larger cities.

Salaries vary depending on how large the plant is. An average salary for a sewage plant operator is about $18,700. Experienced operators can earn up to $27,000. Salaries for supervisors of large plants can top $30,000.

Ways of getting more information

Making a field trip to a local water and wastewater treatment plant would be a good way to learn about this job. A librarian can help you find articles about water pollution and water treatment.

For further information write to the following addresses:

▶ Dipping a sample collector into the treatment tank, a water treatment plant operator checks the quality of the water.

▶ National Environmental Training Association
    8687 Via De Ventura
    Scottsdale, AZ 85258

▶ Superintendent of Documents
    U.S. Government Printing Office
    Washington, DC 20402

▶ Water Pollution Control Federation
    601 Wythe Street
    Alexandria, VA 22314

Welders

Other Articles to Look At:

▶ **Aircraft Mechanics**
▶ **Automobile Mechanics**
▶ **Automotive Body Repairers**
▶ **Forge Shop Occupations**
▶ **Sheet-Metal Workers**

What welders do

The ancient art of welding, which consists of joining two pieces of metal together, has long since adapted the most modern technology for its uses. *Welders* and welding machines join metal by applying heat, pressure, or both, until the edges meet and the pieces are permanently fused. This process is used in the manufacturing and repair of many different products, from water faucets and refrigerators to cars, planes, and missiles.

There are more than forty different welding processes. These procedures can be grouped into three categories: arc welding, gas welding, and resistance welding. In arc welding the workers strikes an arc (that is, creates an electric current) by touching the metal with an electrode. The welder guides the electrode along the metal seams until the heat of the arc melts the metal.

Gas welding is the most commonly used process; its flexibility makes it popular in almost all kinds of metalworking. The flame the welder uses comes from a mixture of oxygen and a combustible gas. To get the right flame size and quality, the welder must adjust the oxygen and gas valves on the torch, then hold the flame against the metal until it melts. The welding rod is then applied to the molten metal to form the weld that holds the pieces together.

Finally, resistance welding gets its heat source from resistance by the workpiece to an electric current and from pressure. Resistance welding is a machine process used in the mass production of various kinds of manufacturing parts.

Education and training

For all welding jobs, employers look for workers who are in good physical condition and have steady hands and good eyesight. For skilled jobs (and this would include maintenance work, where welders travel to construction sites or utility plants to do repairs) a high-school or vocational school diploma is preferred. Classwork should include mathematics, mechanical drawing, physics, and shopwork.

To become a welder, a person must usually complete an on-the-job training program. The length of training time varies from several weeks for most resistance welding jobs to between one and three years for skilled arc and gas welding jobs.

Earnings

The metalworking industry as a whole is growing fast and so there should be a great need for trained welders during the early 1990s and beyond.

Average hourly earnings of welders depend on the skill of the job, as well as on industry or activity in which the welder is employed. The average annual pay for welders in the early 1990s ranged from about $25,000 to $37,440.

Ways of getting more information

To enter the welding trade, applicants should contact a manufacturing plant, the state employment service bureau, or the local branch of the appropriate union.

For more information about the work of welders write to:

▶ American Welding Society
  PO Box 35104
  550 Le Jeune Road, NW
  Miami, FL 33135

▶ International Association of Machinists and Aerospace Workers
  1300 Connecticut Avenue
  Washington, DC 20036

▶ International Union, United Automobile, Aerospace and Agricultural Implement Workers of America
  8000 East Jefferson Avenue
  Detroit, MI 48214

▶ Wearing a protective mask, a welder joins two pieces of metal with a small blowtorch.

Wholesale Sales Workers

Other Articles to Look At:

▶ **Buyers**
▶ **Manufacturers' Sales Representatives**
▶ **Retail Sales Workers**
▶ **Retail Store Managers**
▶ **Shipping and Receiving Clerks**

What wholesale sales workers do

Wholesale sales workers sell products to buyers in retail stores and in commercial or industrial companies. These sales workers do not work for the manufacturer of the products. Instead, they work for wholesaling companies that buy from the manufacturer and sell to the retailer.

Wholesale sales workers may sell a great variety of products. Some sell air conditioners, refrigerators, or freezers. Others may sell all the medicines that a drug company produces. All sales workers, however, try to give their customers as much service and support as possible. For instance, they may help the retail buyer to set up a store display, to plan advertising, and to find out about buying trends. The sales worker may also write up orders, make sure the products are delivered, arrange for payment, prepare reports of sales and expenses, and solve any problems the buyer may have.

Most wholesale sales workers specialize in a certain type of product. Also, many sales workers work in one region or district. By visiting the same customers regularly, they get to know their customers' needs. Much of a wholesale sales worker's time is spent traveling from one customer to another. Some products sell more at one time of year than at another, so that sales workers sometimes suffer periods of low work activity.

Education and training

Wholesale employers prefer to hire applicants who have at least a high-school education. A degree from a junior college can help an applicant get a better job in the wholesale field. Some high-school courses that are useful for future wholesale sales workers are English, bookkeeping, economics, typing, office procedures, and sales-related courses. These make useful college courses, too, as do economics, marketing, wholesaling, retailing, advertising, and accounting. A college degree is often required for jobs in specialized fields. Wholesalers who work with medicines and drugs, for instance, should have a biology degree.

No special licenses are required to work as a wholesale sales worker. Having experience in the wholesale field or in other sales areas is the best way to get a job and to advance. High-school graduates may apply directly to wholesale employers listed in the telephone directory. College graduates or experienced workers in other fields may learn of openings through employment services, guidance counselors, or sales associations.

▶ Placing an order over the phone, a wholesale sales worker obtains items to be sold in large quantities to stores.

Earnings

Throughout the 1990s, wholesale sales workers will have more job opportunities than the average for other professions. Job openings will arise as the population and the economy grow and as new products come into the market.

When wholesale sales workers begin a job, they usually receive either a salary or a combination of salary and commission (a percentage of the price of an item sold). In the early 1990s, wholesale sales workers earned an average of $23,400 a year. Half of them made between $16,640 and $33,800. One-tenth of all sales workers earned less than $12,480, while another one-tenth received over $44,200. Those who have occasional periods of low work activity often are paid a certain amount to get them through that period. Those payments are then subtracted from future commissions.

Ways of getting more information

For more information write to:

▶ National Association of Wholesaler-Distributors
   1725 K Street, NW
   Washington, DC 20006

▶ Sales and Marketing Executives International
   Statler Office Tower, No. 458
   Cleveland, OH 44115

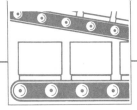

Winemakers

Other Articles to Look At:

▶ **Agricultural Scientists**
▶ **Dietitic Technicians**
▶ **Dietitians**
▶ **Farmers**
▶ **Food Technologists**
▶ **Home Economists**

What winemakers do

Enology—better known as winemaking—is more than 5,000 year old, certainly one of the world's oldest professions. The ancient Egyptians, Greeks, Romans, and Chinese all used wine for either medicinal or religious purposes or just to drink with a meal. Grapes for winemaking have been grown in the United States since the late 1800s and winemaking is now a major industry, especially in California, where more than 80 percent of America's wines are produced.

Winemakers are involved in all phases of wine production and must have a thorough understanding of the business. As an expert in "viticulture," which is another word for the growing of grapes, the enologists has many important decisions to make and perhaps the most important one is which grapes to grow. Winemakers study the different European and native American grapes and then decide which varieties are best for the soil and climate of their land. For example, a winemaker in the Napa Valley of California would need to make sure the grapes planted could withstand very hot summers, while in Upstate New York grapes need to survive extremely cold winters. The variety of grape that's grown determines when to plant, when to prune, and when to pick. The winemaker also has the final work—usually after consulting with staff members—about the testing and crushing of the grapes and their cooling, filtering, and bottling.

As the winery's business manager, a winemaker must have the ability to analyze profit-and-loss statements and other parts of balance sheets. They are also involved with the marketing of the wines, including making such crucial decisions as where the wines will be sold and at what price. Winemakers usually oversee all matters involving their staffs, for example, hiring and firing and setting salaries. Winemakers are top-level managers who have final responsibility for the success of their wineries.

Education and training

Wine-making is an increasingly competitive field and a college degree is often needed to obtain an entry-level job. High-school coursework should emphasize biology, chemistry, and other sciences, and the college major should be in either viticulture or horticulture. In addition, business and computer courses should be a part of the student's college program.

Advancement within the profession depends on a combination of education, experience, and skill. Winemakers at small wineries may move on to become managers of large ones, and they in turn may become directors of several wineries that are part of a large corporation. Because of the small number of wineries, however, and the fact that enologists are already high-level managers, opportunities for advancement are limited.

Earnings

Wine-drinking has become very popular since the 1960s and 1970s and this trend is expected to continue. There should be many job opportunities for prospective winemakers. Most jobs are and will continue to be in California, specifically in the San Joaquin, Napa, and Sonoma valleys.

Beginning salary levels depend on the applicant's education level and the size of the winery. The average beginning salary is between $18,000 and $28,000 per year. Experienced winemakers earn between $30,000 and $85,000 per year.

Ways of getting more information

There are many opportunities for part-time and summer jobs at most good-sized wineries. Working at a winery even for a short time will help a prospective winemaker decide if he or she has the skill and outlook needed for this career. Many wineries give tours, and this is also a useful way to observe the profession close up.

For more information write to the following:

► Testing during the aging process is one of the skills needed by winemakers to make sure the wine is aging well.

► American Society for Enology and Viticulture
 PO Box 1855
 Davis, CA 95617

► American Wine Society
 3006 Latta Road
 Rochester, NY 14612

Wood Science and Technology Careers

Other Articles to Look At:

▶ **Agricultural Engineers**
▶ **Construction Workers**
▶ **Foresters**
▶ **Forestry Technicians**
▶ **Papermaking Occupations**
▶ **Wood Processor Operators**

What wood scientists and technologists do

There are three major career areas in the wood science and technology field. These are *wood scientist, wood technologist,* and *wood products technician.* All three study and test wood and products made out of wood.

Wood scientists try to find new ways to dry, preserve, and make things out of wood. They may develop new ways to dry, or cure, wood so that it will last longer. One way to dry wood planks is to heat them in large ovens called "kilns." Some wood scientists study and improve this heating process. They try to find ways to keep the wood from splitting or bending as it is dried. Other wood scientists develop chemicals that will protect the wood from rotting, insects, or fire. Still others test different kinds of wood to see how they can best be used.

Wood technologists, also called *wood products engineers,* often work for lumber or paper

industries. They test wood-related materials and equipment, such as kilns, sawmill machinery, and pulp machines. They may also test woods for strength and develop new ways to glue wood. Some wood technologists give advice to home builders about what kinds of wood to use for doors, floors, or outdoor decks.

Wood products technicians work for companies that make wood products. They oversee the operation of kilns, saws, wood presses, and other equipment and make sure they are in good working order. Wood products technicians are problem solvers, too. They may run tests on wood to make sure of its quality. Often they give their employers advice on how to process wood more efficiently.

Working conditions for wood science workers vary. Those who do research work in laboratories. Travel is often required for those who buy or sell wood for their employers. Many wood technologists and technicians work in sawmills or processing plants, where the work may be noisy or dirty.

Education and training

Wood scientists and technologists should have a bachelor's degree with a major in forests products or wood technology. Other acceptable degrees are chemistry, engineering, physics, biology, and civil or mechanical engineering. With these degrees, however, it is important to take courses in wood science. Some wood science courses include wood anatomy, wood structure, wood physics, and wood chemistry. Wood products technicians must have a certificate or an associate degree from a two-year college. High-school students interested in a career in wood science or technology should take mathematics, English, and science courses such as physics, chemistry, and biology.

Earnings

Between 1985 and the year 2000, the need for wood products is expected to have doubled. Thus, there will be a tremendous demand for wood scientists, technologists, and technicians throughout the 1990s.

In the early 1990s, wood scientists and technologists with a bachelor's degree earned a beginning salary of about $16,500 to $22,000 a year. Those working for the federal government began at $17,824 and after a long career earned as much as $52,262 a year. Wood scientists and technologists with a doctorate started at $27,500 to $33,000 per year. The average yearly salary for experienced wood products technicians in the early 1990s was about $22,000. Starting salary for these technicians ranged from $13,200 to $17,600 per year.

Ways of getting more information

Young people interested in wood science and technology careers may be able to take a tour or a field trip to a sawmill, paper plant, or wood processing plant in their area. They may also learn about wood and how to work with it through a wood shop or woodworking course in high school or a local vocational school or community college.

▶ A wood scientist stains wood samples to check for damage done to the fibers during processing.

For more information about wood science, wood technology, or forestry careers, write to:

▶ Society of American Foresters
5400 Grosvenor Lane
Bethesda, MD 20814

▶ Society of Wood Science and Technology
PO Box 5062
Madison, WI 53705

Word Processor Operators

Other Articles to Look At:

▶ **Computer Programmers**
▶ **Computer-Service Engineering Technicians**
▶ **Office-Machine Servicers**
▶ **Systems Analysts**
▶ **Typists**

What word processor operators do

Word processor operators use computers to type handwritten or tape-recorded material and put it in final form. Word processor operators can produce letters, legal documents, reports, or charts on their machines. Word processors have a keyboard that looks like the keyboard of a typewriter. Whatever the operator types appears lit up on a screen, much like a small TV screen, called a "video display terminal," or a VDT. As the operator types, the word processor's computer stores the material on a tape or a disk. The operator can correct any mistakes, add things, or make changes instantly to a document before making a final copy.

As the operators type in material, they also type in directions for the computer. For example, some symbols may tell the computer to underline a certain sentence or to put the title in the center of the paper. The operator can have the word processor line up numbers in columns to make a chart, put the material in letter form, or create bar or line graphs.

When the document is typed in, corrected, and arranged in the proper form, the word processor electronically transfers the document to a printer that prints it out. The operator only has to type a document once; the printer can then make as many copies as the operator needs.

If the operators need to send a form letter to hundreds of people, they can direct the word processor to type hundreds of copies of the letter, changing only the address on each one.

All kinds of offices—law firms, government agencies, hospitals, stores and other businesses—employ work processing operators. Operators usually work in comfortable and well-lighted offices, sitting at desks or tables most of the day.

Many operators work thirty-five to forty hours a week although they may have to work overtime on rush projects. Some offices have two work shifts, one during the day and one in the evening, so that they get as much as they can from the machines.

Education and training

Word processor operators must finish high school. High-school courses in typing and using office machines will be useful. Word processor operators also need to be good in grammar and spelling.

Some employers will train new employees on word processors. It takes from three to

▶ Entering information into a computer, a word processor operator prepares a document for storing and reprinting.

six months to become skilled at operating a word processor; operators need to type forty-five to eighty words a minute. Most employers prefer to hire those who have already learned how to use word processors.

Earnings

Throughout the early 1990s, there will be a growing demand for word processor operators in all kinds of businesses.

Beginning word processor operators earn about $13,000 per year. More experienced operators earn $17,000 or more a year. The highest paid workers can make more than $24,000 per year.

Ways of getting more information

For more information write to:

▶ Association of Information Systems Professionals
104 Willmot Road, Suite 201
Deerfield, IL 60015

▶ Data Processing Management Association
505 Busse Highway
Park Ridge, IL 60068

▶ Professional Secretaries International
301 East Armour Boulevard
Kansas City, MO 64111

Writers

Other Articles to Look At:

▶ **Computer Programmers**
▶ **Editors**
▶ **Reporters and Correspondents**
▶ **Technical Writers**

What writers do

Writers express their fictional or factual ideas in written form such as books, magazines, newspapers, reports, newsletters, advertisements, motion pictures, theater, and radio and television broadcasts.

Because the field of writing is so broad, writers usually specialize in a particular type of writing. Those who prepare scripts for motion pictures or television are called *screenwriters*. *Playwrights* do similar writing but for theater. Those who write copy for the purpose of selling goods or services through newspaper or magazine advertisements are called *copywriters*. *Newswriters* prepare stories for newspapers, radio, and TV. *Columnists,* or *commentators,* specialize in writing about things from their personal viewpoints. *Critics* review and comment upon the work of writers, musicians, artists, and performers. In addition to all of these types of writers, there are also *technical writers, novelists, biographers, poets, essayists, comic* and *short story writers*.

Many times authors will write about their own experiences. Sometimes they will select a topic that personally interests them. But most of the time, they are given their writing assignments by the company that has hired them.

Good writers will gather as much information as possible about a subject, and then carefully check the accuracy of their sources. Usually, this involves extensive library research and interviews or long hours of observation and personal experience. Writers keep extensive notes, from which they later prepare an outline. Once the outline has been approved by an editor, an author will write a first draft of the story, or manuscript. Often, the manuscript will have to be rewritten, or revised, several times before it is ready for publication.

Education and training

A college education is necessary if you want to become a writer, as is an ability to type and handle the pressure of deadlines. Some employers prefer to hire people who have a communications or journalism degree. Others require majors in English, literature, history, philosophy, or one of the social sciences. Technical writers should have a background in engineering, business, or one of the sciences.

Earnings

Employment opportunities in writing are very good. Job openings are increasing in the newspaper, motion picture, and broadcasting

▶ A writer reads a lot of material for research on an article.

industries, as well as in the advertising, business and book publishing industries. But competition for jobs in very intense. Those just entering the career will find it difficult to find steady employment.

Beginning writers' salaries range from $16,400 to $20,000 a year. More experienced writers may earn between $23,300 and $31,900. A few best-selling writers may make $100,000 or more per year.

Ways of getting more information

Ask a librarian to help find reference books, such as *Writer's Market* and *Writer's Digest*. They will give helpful hints on how to write and sell manuscripts. Visit a publishing company, newspaper or magazine office and ask the staff writers about their work.

For more information about a career as a writer, contact the following organizations:

▶ Dow Jones Newspaper Fund
   PO Box 300
   Princeton, NJ 08543

▶ Women in Communications
   PO Box 17460
   Arlington, VA 22216

X-Ray Technologists

Other Articles to Look At:

▶ **Biomedical Engineers**
▶ **Electromechanical Technicians**
▶ **Medical Technologists**
▶ **Nuclear Medical Technologists**
▶ **Physicians**
▶ **Registered Nurses**

What X-ray technologists do

X-ray technologists work under the supervision of a physician known as a *radiologist* to help diagnose and treat disease using X rays and radioactive material.

In regular photography, images are made by exposing a specially treated photographic plate to ordinary light rays. In radiography, or X-ray photography, images are made by exposing the plates to special short light rays, called X rays. Because all forms of radiation are potentially harmful, great care must be taken when using X rays. Some X-ray technologists specialize in diagnostic medicine—in figuring out exactly what disease a patient has, and which part of the body it is affecting. These technologists operate the X-ray machines that produce images of bones, tissues, and organs inside the body. When evaluated by the radiologist, the images can be used to locate broken bones, identify diseased tissues, or pinpoint cancerous tumors and other growths.

Other X-ray technologists specialize in

therapeutic work. Radiation therapy uses the effect of radiation to destroy diseased body tissue, and carefully controlled and precisely directed doses of radiation are used to treat some tumors. Working under the direction of radiologists and other physicians, these technologists expose patients to X-rays directed at the diseased body parts.

Some X-ray technologists practice both diagnostic and therapeutic radiology. Others may specialize in such things as nuclear medicine, where radioactive compounds are injected into or swallowed by the patient to diagnose and treat certain conditions, or sonography, where sound waves instead of light waves are used to project an image.

Whatever their specialty, X-ray technologists must be skilled in using potentially dangerous instruments and substances, and must always keep the patient's comfort and safety in mind. And whether employed by hospitals, physicians' and dentists' offices, clinics, laboratories, or government agencies, these workers should be both physically and emotionally healthy themselves, and should have a desire to work with the injured and ill.

Education and training

Prospective X-ray technologists need a high-school education and must then go on to complete a formal education program in radiographic technology. There are currently some 1,020 such programs in the United States, offered by hospitals, medical schools, colleges, and universities, and lasting any-

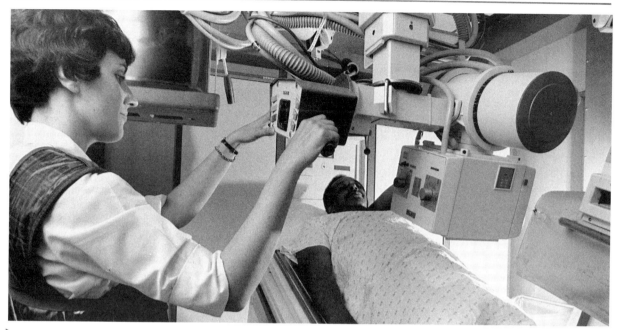

▶ An X-ray technologist positions the machine over the patient.

where from two to four years. Some of these programs require one or two years of higher education beyond high school. And, finally, an increasing number of states have licensing requirements for X-ray technologists, and it is anticipated that in the future all workers will need to be accredited.

Earnings

The future looks excellent for these skilled technologists, as radiology is being used more and more in diagnosing and treating disease.

The starting salary for X-ray technologists in a hospital, medical school, or medical center averaged about $15,700 annually in the early 1990s, while experienced technologists earned up to $26,300 or more.

Ways of getting more information
For more information write to:

▶ American Registry of Radiologic Technologists
2600 Wayzata Boulevard
Minneapolis, MN 55405

▶ American Society of Radiologic Technologists
15000 Central Avenue, SE
Albuquerque, NM 87123

▶ Society of Nuclear Medicine
136 Madison Avenue
New York, NY 10016

Index to Occupational Groupings

Professional Careers

Volume 1	Page
Accountants	12
Actors and Actresses	14
Actuaries	16
Adult and Vocational Education Teachers	18
Aeronautical and Aerospace Technicians	22
Aerospace Engineers	24
Air Traffic Controllers	38
Anthropologists	44
Archaeologists	48
Architects	50
Archivists and Curators	54
Art Directors	56
Artists	58
Assessors and Appraisers	64
Association Executives	66
Astronauts	68
Astronomers	70
Athletes	72
Audio-Control Technicians	78
Audiologists	80
Auditors	84
Authors	86
Bank Officers	108
Biochemists	124
Biologists	126
Biomedical Engineers	128
Buyers	142
CAD/CAM Technicians	146
Cardiac-Monitor Technicians	152
Career Counselors	154
Cartographers	160
Cartoonists and Animators	162
Ceramic Engineers	170
Chemical Engineers	172
Chemical Technicians	174

Chemists	176

Volume 2	Page
Chiropractors	10
Choreographers	12
City Managers	14
City Planners	16
Civil Engineering Technicians	18
Civil Engineers	20
College Administrators	30
College Admissions Directors	32
College and University Faculty	34
College Financial Aid Administrators	36
Commercial Artists	38
Composers	42
Computer Programmers	46
Cost Estimators	66
Creative Directors	72
Crime Lab Technologists	74
Cryptographic Technicians	76
Dancers	82
Data Base Managers	86
Demographers	92
Dental Hygienists	96
Dentists	100
Designers	102
Dialysis Technicians	104
Dietetic Technicians	108
Dietitians	110
Disc Jockeys	112
Dispensing Opticians	114
Display Workers	116
Diving Technicians	118
Drafters	124
Drafting Technicians	126
ECG Technicians	132
Economists	134
Editors	136
EEG Technicians	138
Electrical Engineers	140

Elementary School Teachers	158
Emergency Medical Technicians	162
Employment Counselors	164
Ergonomists	170
Export-Import Specialists	172
Family Practitioners	174

Volume 3	Page
Fashion Designers	16
Field Technicians	22
Food Technologists	46
Foreign-Service Officers	48
Fundraisers	56
Funeral Directors	58
General Managers	70
Geographers	74
Geologists	76
Geophysicists	78
Graphic Arts Technicians	86
Graphics Programmers	88
Guidance Counselors	92
Health Inspectors	96
Historians	104
Home Economists	106
Hospital Administrators	112
Hotel Management	116
Human Services Workers	122
Industrial Designers	128
Industrial Engineers	132
Industrial Traffic Managers	136
Industrial-Safety-and-Health Technicians	138
Information Scientists	142
Interior Designers and Decorators	158
Interpreters	160
Judges	168
Kindergarten Teachers	170
Kinesiotherapists	172
Labor Union Business Agents	176

Volume 4	Page
Lawyers	14
Legal Assistants	20
Librarians	22
Library Assistants	24
Licensed Practical Nurses	26
Light Technicians	30
Linguists	34
Management Analysts	48
Management Trainees	50
Marine Engineers	58
Marketing Researchers	60
Mathematicians	62
Mechanical Engineers	67
Mechanical Technicians	70
Media Planners and Buyers	72
Media Specialists	74
Medical Record Administrators	80
Medical Technologists	84
Merchant Marine Workers	86
Metallurgical Technicians	88
Meteorologists	90
Military Careers	94
Models	102
Museum Occupations	110
Musicians	114
Music Teachers	116
Nuclear Engineers	120
Nuclear Medicine Technologists	124
Nuclear Reactor Operator Technicians	126
Nurse Anesthetists	128
Nurse Practitioners	130
Occupational Therapists	134
Oceanographers	136
Operations-Research Analysts	142
Optometric Technicians	150
Optometrists	152
Orchestra Conductors	154
Osteopathic Physicians	158
Packaging Technicians	160
Packaging Engineers	162

Volume 5	Page
Perfusionists	8
Personnel and Labor Relations Specialists	10
Petroleum Engineers	16
Petrologists	22
Pharmacists	28
Pharmacologists	30
Photographers	34
Physical Radiogical Technicians	40
Physical Therapists	42
Physician Assistants	44
Physicians	46
Physicists	48
Pilots	52
Plastics Technicians	62
Podiatrists	66
Political Scientists	70
Pollution-Control Technicians	72
Polygraph Examiners	74
Preschool Teachers	82
Property and Real Estate Managers	94
Protestant Ministers	98
Psychiatrists	102
Psychologists	104
Public Office Holders	106
Public Relations Specialists	110
Purchasing Agents	112
Rabbis	116
Radio and Telegraph Operators	118
Radio and Television Announcers	120
Radio and Television Newscasters	122
Radio and Television Program Directors	124
Railroad Conductors	128
Recording Industry Workers	136
Recreational Therapists	138
Recreation Workers	140
Registered Nurses	144
Rehabilitation Counselors	146
Reporters	148
Respiratory Therapists	152
Restaurant Managers	154
Roman Catholic Priests	162
School Administrators	172
Scientific and Business Data-Processing Technicians	174

Volume 6	Page
Secondary School Teachers	8
Security Consultants	12
Security Guards	14
Singers	32
Social Workers	36
Sociologists	38
Sound-Recording Technicians	44
Sound Technicians	46
Speech-Language Pathologists	48
Sports Coaches	52
Stage Production Workers	54
Stage Technicians	56
Studio Technicians	72
Surgeons	74
Surgical Technicians	76
Systems Analysts	86
Taxidermists	88
Technical Writers	96
Testing Technicians	106
Toxicologists	124
Umpires	138
Underwriters	140
Veterinarians	146
Video Technicians	148
Writers	166
X-Ray Technologists	168

Clerical Careers

Volume 1	Page
Bank Clerks	106
Bank Tellers	110
Billing Clerks	120
Bookkeepers	134
Cashiers	164

Volume 2	Page
Clerical Supervisors	22
Collection Workers	28
Computer Operators	44
Counter and Retail Clerks	67
Court Reporters	70
Data Entry Clerks	88
Employment Firm Workers	166

Volume 3 — Page
File Clerks — 24
General Office Clerks — 72
Hotel Clerks — 120
Identification Technicians — 124
Insurance Claims
  Representatives — 152
Insurance Policy
  Processing Occupations — 154

Volume 4 — Page
Mail Carriers — 46
Medical Record
  Technicians — 82
Meter Readers — 92

Volume 5 — Page
Postal Clerks — 76
Public Opinion
  Researchers — 108
Railroad Clerks — 126
Receptionists — 134
Reservation Ticket
  Agents — 150

Volume 6 — Page
Secretaries — 10
Shipping and Receiving
  Clerks — 24
Statistical Clerks — 60
Stenographers — 62
Stock Clerks — 67
Switchboard Operators — 84
Tax Preparers — 92
Teacher Aides — 94
Telephone Operators — 104
Title Searchers — 114
Traffic Agents and Clerks — 128
Typists — 136
Word Processor
  Operators — 164

Sales
Careers

Volume 1 — Page
Advertising Sales Workers — 20
Auctioneers — 76
Automobile Sales Workers — 92
Car Rental Agents — 158

Volume 2 — Page
Delivery Drivers — 90
Door-to-Door Sales
  Workers — 122

Volume 4 — Page
Life Insurance Agents — 28
Manufacturers' Sales
  Representatives — 52

Volume 5 — Page
Property and Casualty
  Insurance Agents and
  Brokers — 92
Real Estate Agents — 132
Retail Sales Workers — 156
Retail Store Managers — 158

Volume 6 — Page
Services Sales
  Representatives — 18
Service Station Attendants — 20
Stockbrokers — 66
Telemarketers — 100
Toll Collectors — 118
Travel Agents — 130
Wholesale Sales Workers — 158

Service
Careers

Volume 1 — Page
Athletic Trainers — 74
Audiovisual Technicians — 82
Bakers — 102
Barbers — 112
Bartenders — 114
Bus Drivers — 140
Caterers — 166

Volume 2 — Page
Childcare Workers — 8
Cooks and Chefs — 58
Corrections Officers — 62
Cosmetologists — 64
Dental Assistants — 94
Dog Groomers — 120
Dry Cleaning Workers — 128

Volume 3 — Page
Fast Food Workers — 18
FBI Agents — 20
Fingerprint Classifiers — 26
Fire Control and Safety
  Technicians — 28
Fire Fighters — 30
Flight Attendants — 36
Food Service Workers — 44
Furniture Movers — 62
Gaming Occupations — 66
Homemaker-Home Health
  Aides — 110
Hospital Attendants — 114
Hotel and Motel Workers — 118
Janitors and Cleaners — 164

Volume 4 — Page
Meatcutters — 66
Medical Assistants — 76
Medical-Laboratory
  Technicians — 78
Motion Picture Theater
  Workers — 106
Nannies — 118
Nursing and Psychiatric
  Aides — 132

Volume 5 — Page
Pest Control Workers — 12
Pharmaceutical
  Technicians — 26
Police Officers — 67
Private Household
  Workers — 88
Private Investigators — 90
Psychiatric Technicians — 100
Refuse Collectors — 142

Volume 6 — Page
Shoe Repairers — 28
Ski Lift Operators — 34
State Police Officers — 58
Taxi Drivers — 90
Tour Guides — 122
Truck Drivers — 132
Ushers — 142
Waiters and Waitresses — 150

Agricultural
Careers

Volume 1 — Page
Agribusiness Technicians — 26

Agricultural Engineers	28
Agricultural Equipment Technicians	30
Agricultural Extension Service Workers	32
Agricultural Scientists	34
Animal Health Technicians	40
Animal Production Technicians	42
Beekeepers	116

Volume 2 — **Page**
Coal Mining Technicians	24
Coal Mining Workers	26
Dairy Farmers	78
Energy Use Technicians	168
Farm Crop Production Technicians	176

Volume 3 — **Page**
Farmers	10
Farm Operatives	12
Farriers (Horse Shoers)	14
Fishers, Commercial	32
Fish-Production Technicians	34
Foresters	50
Forestry Technicians	52
Grain Merchants	84
Groundwater Professionals	90

Volume 4 — **Page**
Landscape Architects	8
Landscapers	10
Logging Industry Workers	42
Mining Engineers	98
Ornamental Horticulture Technicians	156
Park Rangers	170
Park Technicians	172

Volume 5 — **Page**
Petroleum Technicians	20
Range Managers	130

Volume 6 — **Page**
Soil Scientists	40
Soil-Conservation Technicians	42
Surveying and Mapping Technicians	78
Surveyors	80
Water Treatment-Plant Operators	154

Wood Science and Technology Careers	162

Processing Careers

Volume 1 — **Page**
Bakery Products Workers	104
Candy Industry Workers	148
Canning Industry Workers	150

Volume 2 — **Page**
Coremakers	60
Dairy Workers	80
Darkroom Technicians	84
Dental-Laboratory Technicians	98
Electroplating Workers	156

Volume 3 — **Page**
Glass Mfg. Workers	80
Heat Treaters	102
Industrial Chemicals Workers	126
Iron and Steel Industry Workers	162

Volume 4 — **Page**
Leather Tanning and Finishing Workers	18
Lithographic Workers	36
Manufacturing Trade Supervisors	54
Meat Packing Workers	64
Molders	104
Paint Industry Workers	164
Papermaking Occupations	168
Pasta Makers	174

Volume 5 — **Page**
Petroleum Drilling Occupations	14
Petroleum Refining Workers	18
Pharmaceutical Industry Workers	24
Photoengravers	32
Photo Lab Workers	38
Plastics Products Manufacturing Workers	60
Printing Press Operators	86

Quality-Control Technicians	114
Rubber Goods Workers	168
Scrap Metal Processing Workers	176

Volume 6 — **Page**
Tobacco Workers	116
Winemakers	160

Machine Careers

Volume 1 — **Page**
Aircraft Mechanics	36
Appliance Repairers	46
Assemblers	62
Automobile-Body Repairers	88
Automobile Mechanics	90
Automotive Engine Technicians	94
Automotive-Exhaust-Emissions Technicians	96
Avionic Technicians	100
Bicycle Mechanics	118
Bindery Workers	122
Brakers	136

Volume 2 — **Page**
Contact Lens Workers	56
Diesel Mechanics	106
Electromechanical Technicians	150

Volume 3 — **Page**
Farm-Equipment Mechanics	8
Flight Engineers	38
Fluid-Power Technicians	42
Forge Shop Workers	54
General Mechanics	67
Gunsmiths	94
Home Electronics Repairers	108
Industrial Electronic Equipment Repairers	130
Industrial Mechanics	134
Instrument Makers	146

Instrumentation
  Technicians 144
Knit Industry Workers 174

Volume 4 **Page**
Locomotive Engineers 40
Machinists 44
Millwrights 96
Mobile Heavy Equipment
  Mechanics 100
Motorcycle Mechanics 108
Nuclear Instrumentation
  Technicians 122
Office-Machine Servicers 138
Patternmakers 176

Volume 5 **Page**
Photographic Equipment
  Technicians 36
Power Plant Workers 80
Prosthetists 96
Robotic Technicians 160
Sawmill Workers 170

Volume 6 **Page**
Textile Technicians 108
Textile Workers 110
Tire Technicians 112
Tool and Die Makers 120
Typesetters 134
Vending-Machine
  Mechanics 144

Bench Work Careers

Volume 1 **Page**
Biomedical Equipment
  Technicians 130

Volume 2 **Page**
Computer-Service
  Technicians 48
Electronics Technicians 152
Electronics Test
  Technicians 154

Volume 3 **Page**
Furniture Upholsterers 64
Furniture Mfg. Workers 60
Instrument Repairers 148
Integrated Circuit
  Technicians 156
Jewelers 166

Volume 4 **Page**
Laser Technicians 12
Locksmiths 38
Musical Instrument
  Repairers 112
Ophthalmic Laboratory
  Technicians 144
Optical Mechanics 146
Optics Technicians 148

Volume 5 **Page**
Piano Technicians 50
Pipe Organ Technicians 56
Pottery Workers 78
Printed-Circuit-Board
  Technicians 84

Volume 6 **Page**
Semiconductor Technicians 16
Shoe Industry Workers 26
Silverware Industry
  Workers 30
Sporting Goods Workers 50
Toy Industry Workers 126
Watch Repairers 152

Structural Careers

Volume 1 **Page**
Architectural Technicians 52
Asphalt Machine
  Operators 60
Automotive Painters 98
Boilermaking Workers 132
Bricklayers 138
Cable-Television
  Technicians 144
Carpenters 156

Cement Masons 168

Volume 2 **Page**
Communications
  Equipment Mechanics 40
Construction Inspectors 50
Construction Supervisors 52
Construction Workers 54
Drywall Installers 130
Electrical Repairers 142
Electrical Technicians 144
Electricians 146
Electric Power Workers 148
Elevator Installers 160

Volume 3 **Page**
Floor Covering Installers 40
Glaziers 82
Heating and Cooling
  Mechanics 98
Heating and Cooling
  Technicians 100
Industrial-truck Operators 140
Insulation Workers 150

Volume 4 **Page**
Layout Workers 16
Line Installers and Cable
  Splicers 32
Marble Setters 56
Operating Engineers 140
Painters and Paperhangers 166

Volume 5 **Page**
Pipefitters 54
Plasterers 58
Plumbers 64
Roofers 164
Roustabouts 166

Volume 6 **Page**
Sheet-Metal Workers 22
Stevedores 64
Structural-Steel Workers 70
Swimming-Pool Servicers 82
Telecommunications
  Technicians 98
Telephone Installers 102
Welders 156

Glossary

accreditation The result of being accredited (see **accredited**). Accreditation of a school or training program is an important indication of the quality of education that students receive. Compare **certification.**

accredited Approved as meeting established standards for providing good training and education. This approval is usually given by an independent organization of professionals to a school or a program in a school. Compare **certified** and **licensed.**

administrative Having to do with managing and directing a business or similar organization.

apprentice A person who is learning a trade by working under the supervision of a skilled worker. Apprentices often receive classroom instruction in addition to their supervised practical experience.

apprenticeship **1.** A program for training apprentices (see **apprentice**). **2.** The period of time when a person is an apprentice. In highly skilled trades, apprenticeships may last three or four years.

aptitude A person's natural inclinations or ability to do something; talent.

assistant A worker whose job is to help in an activity. In some technical fields, an assistant is a worker with some specialized training but less than that of a technician.

associate degree An academic rank or title granted by a community or junior college or similar institution to graduates of a two-year program of education beyond high school.

bachelor's degree An academic rank or title given to a person who has completed a four-year program of study at a college or university. Also called an *undergraduate degree.*

certification The result of being certified (see **certified**). In some fields, certification of workers is highly recommended or required for most jobs. Compare **accreditation.**

certified Approved as meeting established requirements for skill, knowledge, and experience in a particular field. People are certified by the organization of professionals in their field. Compare **accredited** and **licensed.**

commission A percentage of the money taken in by a company in sales that is given to the salesperson as pay, either in addition to or instead of a salary.

Career Day At a high school, a day when representatives of businesses and industries present information to students and answer questions about different types of jobs.

community college A public two-year college, attended by students who do not live at the college. Graduates of a community college receive an associate degree and may transfer to a four-year college or university to complete a bachelor's degree. Compare **junior college** and **technical community college.**

curriculum All the courses available in a school or college; or, the courses offered in a particular subject.

degree An academic title given by a college or university to a student who has completed a program of study.

diploma A certificate or document given by a school to show that a person has completed a course or has graduated from the school.

doctorate An academic rank or title (the highest) granted by a graduate school to a person who has completed a two- to three-year program after having received a master's degree.

earnings Money that a person receives for services given, such as wages, salary, or commission.

engineer **1.** A person (such as a train engineer) who is in charge of running engines or machinery. **2.** A person who is trained in engineering (see **engineering**).

engineering The profession that is concerned with ways of making practical use of scientific knowledge. Typical engineering activities include planning and managing the building of bridges, dams, roads, chemical plants, machinery, and new industrial products.

economy The system in a country, region, or local area for producing, distributing, and using goods and services.

fringe benefit A payment or benefit to an employee in addition to regular wages or salary. Examples of fringe benefits include a pension, a paid vacation, and health or life insurance.

graduate school A school that people may attend after they have received their bachelor's degree. People who successfully complete an educational program at a graduate school earn a master's degree or a doctorate.

guidance counselor A staff member at a school who gives advice to students to help them make personal and educational choices.

humanities The branches of learning that are concerned with language, the arts, literature, philosophy, and history. Compare **social sciences** and **natural sciences.**

intern An advanced student (usually one with at least some college training) in a professional field who is employed in a job that is intended to provide supervised practical experience to the student.

internship 1. The position or job of an intern (see **intern**). 2. The period of time when a person is an intern.

journeyman A person who has completed an apprenticeship or other training period and is qualified to work in a trade.

junior college A two-year college that offers courses like those in the first half of a four-year college program. Graduates of a junior college usually receive an associate degree and may transfer to a four-year college or university to complete a bachelor's degree. Compare **community college.**

labor 1. Employees of a company other than those in management. 2. The organizations (such as unions) representing groups of employees.

liberal arts The subjects covered by college courses that develop broad general knowledge rather than specific occupational skills. The liberal arts are often considered to include philosophy, literature and the arts, history, language, and some courses in the social sciences and natural sciences.

licensed Having formal permission from the proper authority to carry out an activity that would be illegal without that permission. For example, a person may be licensed to practice medicine or to drive a car. Compare **certified.**

life sciences The natural sciences that are concerned with living organisms and the processes that take place within them (see **natural sciences**).

major (in college) The academic field in which a student specializes and receives a degree.

management The employees of a company or institution who control or direct its business affairs. Compare **labor.**

managerial Having to do with management (see **management**).

master's degree An academic rank or title granted by a graduate school to a person who has completed a one- or two-year program after having received a bachelor's degree.

minimum wage The wage established by law as the lowest that may be paid to workers in a particular category.

minority A group of people who make up less than half the population and who differ from the rest of the population especially in regards to race, religion, or ethnic background.

natural sciences All the sciences that are concerned with the objects and processes in nature that can be measured. The natural sciences include biology, chemistry, physics, astronomy, and geology. Compare **humanities** and **social sciences.**

pension An amount of money paid regularly by an employer to a former employee after he or she retires from working.

personnel 1. The group of people who are employed in a company or institution. 2. The department within an organization that is concerned with employees, especially hiring them.

physical sciences The natural sciences that are concerned mainly with nonliving matter, including physics, chemistry, and astronomy.

private 1. Not owned or controlled by the government (such as private industry or a private employment agency). 2. Intended only for a particular person or group; not open to all (such as a private road or a private club).

profession An occupation such as law, medicine, or engineering that requires much education and training.

professional (adjective) 1. Having to do with a profession (see **profession**). 2. Taking part in an activity as a job (such as a professional athlete or a professional actor).

professional (noun) A person who works in a profession (see **profession**).

public **1.** Provided or operated by the government (such as a public library). **2.** Open and available to everyone (such as public meeting).

regulatory Having to do with the rules and laws for carrying out an activity. A regulatory agency, for example, is a government organization that sets up required procedures for how certain things should be done.

retail Engaged in selling goods, usually in small amounts, directly to the people who will use the goods. Compare **wholesale.**

salary A set amount of money periodically paid to a person in return for work that the person regularly does.

scholarship A gift of money to a student to help the student pay for further education.

social sciences The branches of learning (such as economics and political science) that are concerned with the behavior of groups of human beings. Compare **humanities** and **natural sciences.**

social studies Courses of study (such as civics, geography, and history) that deal with how human societies work.

specifications Precise and detailed plans, diagrams, or instructions that describe exactly how something is to be done.

starting salary The salary paid to a newly hired employee. The starting salary is usually a smaller amount than is paid to a more experienced worker.

supervise To direct or have charge of a project or a group of people.

technical college A private or public college offering two- or four-year programs in technical subjects. Technical colleges offer courses in both general and technical subjects and award associate degrees and bachelor's degree. Compare **technical community college.**

technical community college A community college that provides training for technicians (see **community college**). Technical community colleges offer courses in both general and technical subjects and award associate degrees. Compare **technical college.**

technical institute A public or private school that offers training in technical subjects. Technical institutes usually offer only a few courses in general subjects and do not award any kind of degree. Technical institutes that offer a broader range of subjects and award degrees are usually called **technical colleges** or **technical community colleges.**

technical school A general term used to describe technical colleges, technical community colleges, and technical institutes. Compare **trade school** and **vocational school.**

technician A worker with specialized practical training in a mechanical or scientific subject who works under the supervision of scientists, engineers, or other professionals. Technicians typically receive two years of college-level education after high school.

technologist A worker in a mechanical or scientific field with more training than a technician. Technologists typically must have between two and four years of college-level education after high school.

trade An occupation that requires training and skills in working with one's hands.

trade school A public or private school that offers training in one or more of the trades (see **trade**). Compare **technical school** and **vocational school.**

undergraduate A student at a college or university who has not yet received a degree.

undergraduate degree See **bachelor's degree.**

union An organization whose members are workers in a particular industry or company. The union works to gain better wages, benefits, and working conditions for its members. Also called a *labor union* or *trade union.*

vocational school A public or private school that offers training in one or more skills or trades. Compare **technical school** and **trade school.**

wage Money that is paid in return for work done, especially money paid on the basis of the number of hours or days worked.

wholesale Engaged in selling goods, usually in large amounts, to retail dealers. Compare **retail.**

Photo Credits

Page   Credit

VOLUME 1

Page	Credit
13	H. Armstrong Roberts
15	Brian Seed, TSW-Click/Chicago
17	H. Armstrong Roberts
19	Camerique
21	Paul Merideth, TSW-Click/Chicago
23	NASA
25	NASA
27	John Deere & Company
29	U.S. Dept. of Agriculture
31	John Deere & Company
33	U.S. Dept. of Agriculture
35	U.S. Dept. of Agriculture
37	American Airlines
39	IBM
41	David Strickler, TSW-Click/Chicago
43	U.S. Dept. of Agriculture
45	SUNY at Buffalo
47	General Electric
49	Robert Frerck, TSW-Click/Chicago
51	Matt Ferguson
53	Richard Younker, TSW-Click/Chicago
55	Paul Merideth, TSW-Click/Chicago
57	Paul Merideth, TSW-Click/Chicago
59	H. Armstrong Roberts
61	Barber-Green Company
63	Paul Merideth, TSW-Click/Chicago
65	Charles Gupton, TSW-Click/Chicago
67	Camerique
69	NASA
71	John Darby, UIC
73	Paul Merideth, TSW-Click/Chicago
75	Mary E. Messenger
77	Jim Pickerell, TSW-Click/Chicago
79	WGBH Boston
81	Academy of Dispensing Audiologists
83	H. Armstrong Roberts
85	Allstate
87	Paul Merideth, TSW-Click/Chicago
89	MAACO
91	David Strickler, TSW-Click/Chicago
93	H. Armstrong Roberts
95	IBM
97	Bob Wiatrolik, Illinois EPA
99	Nat'l Inst. for Auto. Serv. Excellence
101	Honeywell, Inc.
103	H. Armstrong Roberts
105	Mary E. Messenger
107	Charles Gupton, TSW-Click/Chicago
109	Camerique
111	Camerique
113	Camerique
115	Paul Merideth, TSW-Click/Chicago
117	Mary E. Messenger
119	Mary E. Messenger
121	Wayne Michael Lottinville
123	R. R. Donnelley & Sons
125	U.S. Dept. of Agriculture
127	Val vonSchacht, UIC
129	Wright State University
131	Mary E. Messenger
133	Dave Lawsen
135	Paul Merideth, TSW-Click/Chicago
137	Santa Fe Railroad
139	Camerique
141	Richard Younker, TSW-Click/Chicago
143	Richard Younker, TSW-Click/Chicago
145	David Joel, TSW-Click/Chicago
147	H. Armstrong Roberts
149	Hershey Foods Corporation
151	H. Armstrong Roberts
153	Jim Pickerell, TSW-Click/Chicago
155	John Darby, UIC
157	H. Armstrong Roberts
159	Wayne Michael Lottinville
161	Rand McNally & Company
163	David R. Frazier Photolibrary
165	IBM
167	Marriott Corporation
169	Matt Ferguson
171	Coors Ceramics Company
173	IBM
175	H. Armstrong Roberts
177	American Electroplaters & Surface Finishers Society

VOLUME 2

Page	Credit
9	Wayne Michael Lottinville
11	Art Stein, Am. Chiropractic Assoc.
13	Mark Reinstein, TSW-Click/Chicago
15	Wayne Michael Lottinville
17	Paul Merideth, TSW-Click/Chicago
19	Peter LeGrand, TSW-Click/Chicago
21	H. Armstrong Roberts
23	Camerique
25	Consolidation Coal Company
27	Consolidation Coal Company
29	American Airlines
31	Val vonSchacht, UIC
33	Val vonSchacht, UIC
35	Mary Carm, UIC
37	John Darby, UIC
39	Paul Merideth, TSW-Click/Chicago
41	AT&T
43	Paul Merideth, TSW-Click/Chicago
45	Hewlett Packard
47	IBM
49	H. Armstrong Roberts
51	H. Armstrong Roberts
53	John Lawlor, TSW-Click/Chicago
55	Richard Younker, TSW-Click/Chicago
57	Herley Bouwens, Bausch & Lomb
59	H. Armstrong Roberts
61	American Foundrymen's Society
63	Illinois Dept. of Corrections
65	H. Armstrong Roberts
67	Lawrence Manning, TSW-Click
69	Robert Frerck, TSW-Click/Chicago
71	Stenograph Corporation
73	H. Armstrong Roberts
75	Chicago Police Department
77	IBM
79	U.S. Dept. of Agriculture
81	Paul Damien, TSW-Click/Chicago
83	Paul Merideth, TSW-Click/Chicago
85	Camerique
87	IBM
89	Camerique
91	Woods Hole Oceanographic Institute
93	UPS
95	Val vonSchacht, UIC
97	American Dental Association
99	Mary Carm, UIC
101	Mary Carm, UIC
103	American Dental Association
105	H. Armstrong Roberts
107	Steve Goldberg
109	Wayne Michael Lottinville
111	John Darby, UIC
113	Matt Ferguson
115	Mary E. Messenger
117	Pearle Vision Center
119	Kenneth Hayden, TSW-Click/Chicago
121	Mary E. Messenger
123	Avon
125	H. Armstrong Roberts
127	Tennessee Valley Authority
129	Robert Frerck, TSW-Click/Chicago
131	H. Armstrong Roberts
133	Shearson Lehman Hutton
135	H. Armstrong Roberts
137	Art Plotnik
139	Jim Pickerell, TSW-Click/Chicago
141	Honeywell, Inc.
143	Commonwealth Edison
145	Honeywell, Inc.

Page	Credit
147	M. Elenz-Traner
149	Commonwealth Edison
151	IBM
153	Zenith Corporation
155	Zenith Corporation
157	Am. Electroplaters Society
159	Camerique
161	Otis Elevator
163	Camerique
165	Jim Pickerell, TSW-Click/Chicago
167	Snelling & Snelling
169	Wayne Michael Lottinville
171	Dr. W. Karwowski
173	ENESCO
175	Camerique
177	U.S. Dept. of Agriculture

VOLUME 3

Page	Credit
9	U.S. Dept. of Agriculture
11	U.S. Dept. of Agriculture
13	U.S. Dept. of Agriculture
15	Mary E. Messenger
17	Paul Merideth, TSW-Click/Chicago
19	David R. Frazier Photolibrary
21	Paul Merideth, TSW-Click/Chicago
23	H. Armstrong Roberts
25	Charles Gupton, TSW-Click/Chicago
27	Chicago Police Department
29	H. Armstrong Roberts
31	Camerique
33	H. Armstrong Roberts
35	Delta Pride Catfish, Inc.
37	American Airlines
39	American Airlines
41	Matt Ferguson
43	Parker Hannifin Corporation
45	American Airlines
47	American Bakers Association
49	no credit
51	H. Armstrong Roberts
53	Camerique
55	American Iron & Steel Institute
57	John Coletti, TSW-Click/Chicago
59	Mary E. Messenger
61	H. Armstrong Roberts
63	North American Van Lines
65	Wayne Michael Lottinville
67	Hilton Hotels Corporation
69	Santa Fe Railroad
71	H. Armstrong Roberts
73	Al Henderson, TSW-Click/Chicago
75	IBM
77	E. F. Patterson III
79	IBM
81	Frank Petronio, Steuben Glassworks
83	Service Glass Company
85	U.S. Dept. of Agriculture
87	John Darby, UIC
89	Charles Gupton, TSW-Click/Chicago
91	*Water Well Journal*

Page	Credit
93	J. Nettis, H. Armstrong Roberts
95	Mary E. Messenger
97	Paul Merideth, TSW-Click/Chicago
99	Camerique
101	Mary Carm, UIC
103	Lindberg Corporation
105	Peter LeGrand, TSW-Click/Chicago
107	Val vonSchacht, UIC
109	David R. Frazier Photolibrary
111	Mathew Neal McVay, TSW-Click
113	John Darby, UIC
115	John Darby, UIC
117	Loren Santow, TSW-Click/Chicago
119	Marriott Corporation
121	Marriott Corporation
123	Paul Merideth, TSW-Click/Chicago
125	Chicago Police Department
127	Bob Thomason, TSW-Click/Chicago
129	IBM
131	H. Armstrong Roberts
133	Honeywell, Inc.
135	Mary E. Messenger
137	H. Armstrong Roberts
139	Mary E. Messenger
141	Mary E. Messenger
143	Val vonSchacht, UIC
145	Honeywell, Inc.
147	Honeywell, Inc.
149	Honeywell, Inc.
151	H. Armstrong Roberts
153	Wayne Michael Lottinville
155	Allstate
157	H. Armstrong Roberts
159	Am. Soc. of Interior Designers
161	United Nations
163	Michael Hayman, TSW-Click/Chicago
165	Marriott Corporation
167	H. Armstrong Roberts
169	H. Armstrong Roberts
171	Camerique
173	Val vonSchacht, Inc.
175	Labor Unity
177	Don Smetzer, TSW-Click/Chicago

VOLUME 4

Page	Credit
9	Wayne Michael Lottinville
11	Gary Irving, The Morton Arboretum
13	Honeywell, Inc.
15	Paul Merideth, TSW-Click/Chicago
17	H. Armstrong Roberts
19	Pfister & Vogel Tanning Co.
21	Wayne Michael Lottinville
23	H. Armstrong Roberts
25	H. Armstrong Roberts
27	Paul Damien, TSW-Click/Chicago
29	Allstate
31	Wayne Michael Lottinville
33	Billy E. Barnes, TSW-Click/Chicago
35	Val vonSchacht, UIC
37	Henley & Savage, TSW-Click/Chicago

Page	Credit
39	Associated Locksmiths of America
41	Santa Fe Railroad
43	Weyerhaeuser Corporation
45	John Deere & Company
47	U.S. Postal Service
49	H. Armstrong Roberts
51	IBM
53	Paul Merideth, TSW-Click/Chicago
55	David R. Frazier Photolibrary
57	H. Armstrong Roberts
59	Wayne Michael Lottinville
61	IBM
63	Wayne Michael Lottinville
65	Richard Younker, TSW-Click/Chicago
67	Mary E. Messenger
69	Grumman Corporation
71	Grumman Corporation
73	Vic Bider, TSW-Click/Corporation
75	Camerique
77	Camerique
79	John Darby, UIC
81	Am. Medical Records Assoc.
83	Am. Medical Records Assoc.
85	Peter LeGrand, TSW-Click/Chicago
87	Lee Klima
89	Bruce Taylor, Alfred University
91	L.L.T. Rhodes, TSW-Click/Chicago
93	Commonwealth Edison
95	Michael Hayman, TSW-Click/Chicago
97	Michael Mauney, TSW-Click/Chicago
99	Consolidation Coal Company
101	Michael Hayman, TSW-Click/Chicago
103	Paul Merideth, TSW Click/Chicago
105	American Foundrymen's Society
107	Theater Equipment Association
109	Motorcycle Mechanic Institute
111	Paul Merideth, TSW-Click/Chicago
113	Wayne Michael Lottinville
115	Cary Wolinski, TSW-Click/Chicago
117	Paul Merideth, TSW-Click/Chicago
119	National Academy of Nannies
121	Tennessee Valley Authority
123	Commonwealth Edison
125	Rush-Presbyterian-St. Lukes
127	Commonwealth Edison
129	L.L.T. Rhodes, TSW-Click/Chicago
131	Paul Damien, TSW-Click/Chicago
133	Paul Damien, TSW-Click/Chicago
135	H. Armstrong Roberts
137	Woods Hole Oceanographic Institute
139	Wayne Michael Lottinville
141	Consolidation Coal Company
143	Hewlett Packard
145	Wayne Michael Lottinville
147	Itek Optical Systems
149	Pearle Vision Center
151	John Darby, UIC
153	Pearle Vision Center
155	Paul Merideth, TSW-Click/Chicago
157	UIC

Page	Credit
159	Kim Sokoloff, Am. Osteopathic Assoc.
161	Weyerhaeuser Corporation
163	Jefferson Smurfit Corporation
165	Benjamin Moore Paints
167	Matt Ferguson
169	Weyerhaeuser Corporation
171	David Strickler, TSW-Click/Chicago
173	Illinois Dept. of Conservation
175	Hershey Foods Corporation
177	American Foundrymen's Society

VOLUME 5

Page	Credit
9	© Sarns, 3M Health Group
11	IBM
13	Camerique
15	American Petroleum Institute
17	Amoco Corporation
19	American Petroleum Institute
21	Amoco Corporation
23	IBM
25	The UpJohn Company
27	John Darby, UIC
29	Val vonSchacht, UIC
31	Mary E. Messenger
33	H. Armstrong Roberts
35	Camerique
37	Mary E. Messenger
39	Diane Graham-Henry
41	David R. Fraizer Photography
43	H. Armstrong Roberts
45	Am. Acad. of Physician Assistants
47	H. Armstrong Roberts
49	Honeywell, Inc.
51	Michael Hayman, TSW-Click/Chicago
53	H. Armstrong Roberts
55	Pipe Industry Fund
57	Wicks Organ Company
59	Mary E. Messenger
61	H. Armstrong Roberts
63	DuPont Corporation
65	Peter LeGrand, TSW-Click/Chicago
67	Scholl School of Podiatric Medicine
69	H. Armstrong Roberts
71	Paul Merideth, TSW-Click/Chicago
73	Richard Younker, TSW-Click/Chicago
75	Chicago Police Department
77	H. Armstrong Roberts
79	Bennington Potters, Inc.
81	David Falconer
83	H. Armstrong Roberts
85	Hewlett Packard
87	R. R. Donnelley & Sons
89	Wayne Michael Lottinville
91	David R. Frazier Photolibrary
93	Allstate
95	David R. Frazier Photolibrary
97	Orthotics & Prosthetics Nat'l Of.
99	Paul Merideth, TSW-Click/Chicago
101	Paul Damien, TSW-Click/Chicago
103	Stacy Pickerell, TSW-Click/Chicago

Page	Credit
105	John Darby, UIC
107	H. Armstrong Roberts
109	Mary E. Messenger
111	Jim Pickerell, TSW-Click/Chicago
113	Santa Fe Railroad
115	IBM
117	Paul Merideth, TSW-Click/Chicago
119	IBM
121	Paul Merideth, TSW-Click/Chicago
123	Kelly Mills, TBS, Inc.
125	Paul Merideth, TSW-Click/Chicago
127	Santa Fe Railroad
129	Matt Ferguson
131	U.S. Dept. of Agriculture
133	H. Armstrong Roberts
135	Jim Pickerell, TSW-Click/Chicago
137	Wide World
139	Mary E. Messenger
141	Wayne Michael Lottinville
143	Mary E. Messenger
145	Camerique
147	Oscar H. Izquierdo, Rehabilitation Institute of Chicago
149	Mark Reinstein, TSW-Click/Chicago
151	American Airlines
153	Am. Assoc. for Respiratory Care
155	H. Armstrong Roberts
157	H. Armstrong Roberts
159	IBM
161	John Deere & Company
163	Barbara Van Cleve, TSW-Click
165	Paul Merideth, TSW-Click/Chicago
167	American Petroleum Institute
169	Goodyear
171	Weyerhaeuser Corporation
173	Wayne Michael Lottinville
175	IBM
177	Paul Merideth, TSW-Click/Chicago

VOLUME 6

Page	Credit
9	IBM
11	IBM
13	Camerique
15	Mary E. Messenger
17	Honeywell, Inc.
19	IBM
21	David Strickler, TSW-Click/Chicago
23	Sheet Metal National Association
25	Camerique
27	Allen Edmonds
29	Mary E. Messenger
31	Reed & Barton Silversmiths
33	H. Armstrong Roberts
35	David Lokey
37	John Darby, UIC
39	H. Armstrong Roberts
41	Consolidation Coal Company
43	U.S. Dept. of Agriculture
45	David R. Frazier Photolibrary
47	WGBH Boston

Page	Credit
49	IBM
51	Wilson Sporting Goods Co.
53	Mary E. Messenger
55	David Falconer, David R. Frazier
57	Wayne Michael Lottinville
59	Illinois State Police
61	IBM
63	IBM
65	Paul Merideth, TSW-Click/Chicago
67	David R. Frazier Photolibrary
69	Paul Merideth, TSW-Click/Chicago
71	Richard Younker, TSW-Click/Chicago
73	WGBH Boston
75	Paul Damien, TSW-Click/Chicago
77	John Darby, UIC
79	Peter LeGrand, TSW-Click/Chicago
81	Camerique
83	Mary E. Messenger
85	AT&T
87	IBM
89	Wayne Michael Lottinville
91	Mary E. Messenger
93	Mary E. Messenger
95	David R. Frazier Photolibrary
97	Val vonSchacht, UIC
99	AT&T
101	Charles Gupton, TSW-Click/Chicago
103	Pacific Bell
105	Pacific Bell
107	Harvey Phillips, TSW-Click/Chicago
109	IBM
111	Am. Textile Mfg. Inst.
113	Goodyear
115	Allstate
117	Charles Buchanan
119	Illinois State Toll Highway Authority
121	Gerry Sauter, TSW-Click/Chicago
123	David R. Frazier Photolibrary
125	FBI
127	Crisloid, Inc.
129	IBM
131	H. Armstrong Roberts
133	H. Armstrong Roberts
135	Mary E. Messenger
137	Val vonSchacht, UIC
139	Mary E. Messenger
141	Allstate
143	David R. Frazier Photolibrary
145	Canteen Corporation
147	H. Armstrong Roberts
149	WGBH Boston
151	Marriott Corporation
153	David R. Frazier Photolibrary
155	Water Reclamation District
157	Billy E. Barnes, TSW-Click/Chicago
159	Paul Merideth, TSW-Click/Chicago
161	Robert Mondavi Winery
163	Inst. of Paper Science & Tech.
165	Hewlett Packard
167	Paul Merideth, TSW-Click/Chicago
169	Peter LeGrand, TSW-Click/Chicago

Index

Able seamen, **4**:86
Accountants, **1**:12. *See also* Auditors; Billing clerks
Account executives, **1**:20, **6**:66
Accounting clerks, **1**:134
Actors and actresses, **1**:14
Actuaries, **1**:16
Administrators, **1**:66, **2**:32, **2**:36, **4**:48, **4**:50
Admissions directors, **2**:30
Adult and vocational education teachers, **1**:18
Adult education teachers, **1**:18, **1**:32
Advertising industry, **1**:56, **1**:58, **2**:72, **4**:60, **4**:72
Advertising sales workers, **1**:20
Aerial photographers, **5**:34
Aeronautical and aerospace technicians, **1**:22
Aerospace engineers, **1**:24
Aerospace industry, **1**:100, **3**:146, **4**:44
Agents. *See* Labor union business agents
Agribusiness technicians, **1**:26
Agricultural engineers, **1**:28
Agricultural equipment technicians, **1**:30
Agricultural extension service workers, **1**:32
Agricultural inspectors, **3**:96
Agricultural laboratories, **1**:34
Agricultural scientists, **1**:34
Agriculture, **1**:26, **1**:32
Agronomists, **1**:34, **6**:40
Air-conditioning, heating and refrigeration technicians, **3**:100
Air-conditioning and refrigeration mechanics, **3**:98
Aircraft, **1**:24

Aircraft mechanics, **1**:36
Air Force, **4**:94. *See also* Military careers
Airline pilots. *See* Pilots
Airline radio operators, **5**:118
Airlines. *See* Flight attendants
Airline security representatives, **6**:14
Airline stewardesses. *See* Flight attendants
Airplanes, **1**:22, **3**:38. *See also* Air traffic controllers; Astronauts; Pilots
Air pollution-control technicians, **5**:72
Airports, **1**:38
Air-safety inspectors, **3**:96
Air traffic controllers, **1**:38
Alcohol, tobacco, firearms inspectors, **3**:96
Ambulance drivers, **2**:162
Anesthesiology, **4**:128
Animal caretakers, **2**:120
Animal doctors, **6**:146
Animal feeding systems, **1**:30
Animal health technicians, **1**:40
Animal husbandry, **1**:42
Animal production technicians, **1**:42
Animal research, **1**:34, **1**:40
Animals. *See* Livestock management; Veterinarians
Animators, **1**:162, **2**:38
Anthropologists, **1**:44
Apartment building managers, **5**:94
Apparel industry, **3**:174, **4**:102, **6**:108, **6**:110
Applications programmers, **2**:46
Apprenticeships, **1**:60, **1**:104
Archaeologists, **1**:48

Architects, **1**:50
Architectural and building construction technicians, **1**:52
Architectural technicians, **1**:52
Archivists and curators, **1**:54
Armed forces. *See* Military careers
Armored-car guards, **6**:14
Army, **4**:94
Arrival controllers, **1**:38
Art directors, **1**:56
Artificial limb manufacturing, **5**:96
Artists, **1**:58. *See also* Cartoonists
Art restoration workers, **4**:110
Art therapists, **5**:138
Asphalt paving machine operators, **1**:60
Assemblers, **1**:62
Assessors and appraisers, **1**:64
Association executives, **1**:66
Astronauts, **1**:68
Astronomers, **1**:70
Astrophysicists, **1**:70
Athletes, **1**:72, **6**:52
Athletic directors, **2**:32
Athletic equipment, **6**:50
Athletic trainers, **1**:74
Auctioneers, **1**:76
Audio-control technicians, **1**:78
Audiologists, **1**:80
Audio recording technicians, **5**:136
Audiovisual technicians, **1**:82
Auditors, **1**:84
Authors, **1**:86; **6**:166. *See also* Writers
Automated equipment technicians, **4**:160

Automobile auctioneers, **1**:76
Automobile-body repairers, **1**:88
Automobile dealers, **1**:92, **1**:98
Automobile mechanics, **1**:90. *See also* Service station attendants
Automobile rental agents, **1**:158
Automobile sale workers, **1**:92
Automobile workers, **4**:44
Automotive, diesel, and gas turbine technicians, **1**:94
Automotive engineers, **1**:94, **4**:68
Automotive-exhaust-emissions technicians, **1**:96
Automotive mechanics, **1**:18
Automotive painters, **1**:98
Auxiliary-equipment operators, **5**:80
Avionics technicians, **1**:100

Babysitters, **2**:8, **4**:118
Back pain, **2**:10
Bakers, **1**:102
Bakery products workers, **1**:104
Bank clerks, **1**:106
Bank examiners, **3**:96
Bank officers and managers, **1**:108
Bank tellers, **1**:110
Barbers, **1**:112
Barker operators, **4**:168
Bartenders, **1**:114, **6**:150
Baseball glove shapers, **6**:50
Base fillers, **6**:50
Beater engineers, **4**:168
Beauticians, **1**:112

181

Beauty salon
workers, **1**:112
Beekeepers, **1**:116, **3**:10
Bellhops, **3**:118
Bench assemblers, **1**:62
Bicycle mechanics, **1**:118
Bill collectors, **2**:28
Billing clerks, **1**:120
Bindery workers, **1**:122
Biochemists, **1**:124
Biographers, **3**:104; **6**:166.
See also Historians;
Writers
Biologists, **1**:126
Biomedical engineers, **1**:128
Biomedical equipment
technicians, **1**:130
Biomedicine, **1**:124
Blacksmiths, **3**:14
Blast-furnace helpers, **3**:162
Boat building, **4**:58
Boating. *See* Fishers,
commercial
Boat motor repairers, **4**:108
Bodyguards, **5**:90, **6**:12
Boilermaking
workers, **1**:132
Boiler operators, **5**:80
Book binding, **1**:122
Book editors, **2**:136
Bookies, **3**:66
Bookkeepers, **1**:32, **1**:134.
See also Accountants;
Auditors
Book publishing. *See* Graphic
arts technicians;
Typesetters
Books. *See* Authors; Writers
Bouncers, **6**:14
Bowling ball
engravers, **6**:50
Box-office cashiers, **4**:106
Brace manufacturing, **5**:96
Brakemen. *See*
Brakers Brakers, **1**:136
Breeding animals, **1**:42
Bricklayers and
stonemasons, **1**:138
Broadcast employees, **4**:30,
6:148
Broadcasters, **5**:120, **5**:122
Broadcast production
technicians, **6**:72
Broadcast technicians, **6**:44
Broadcast workers, **3**:22

Builders. *See* Architects;
Building construction
technicians
Building construction
technicians, **1**:52
Building industry, **1**:52,
1:138, **1**:156, **2**:52, **2**:54,
2:146, **3**:67, **3**:150, **4**:56,
4:166, **5**:58, **5**:64, **5**:164
Building inspectors, **2**:50
Building maintenance, **3**:67
Bulldozer operators, **4**:140
Bus drivers, **1**:140
Business
administration, **3**:70
Business agents, **3**:176
Butchers, **4**:66
Butlers, **5**:88
Buyers, **1**:142, **5**:112

Cabinetmakers, **3**:60
Cable splicers, **2**:148
Cable-television
technicians, **1**:144
CAD/CAM
technicians, **1**:146
Cafeteria workers, **3**:44
Cake decorators, **1**:102
Camera operators, **3**:86
Camp counselors, **5**:140
Candy industry
workers, **1**:148
Canning and preserving
industry workers, **1**:150
Canning industry
workers, **1**:150
Captains (ships), **4**:86
Car checkers, **6**:24
Cardiac-monitor
technicians, **1**:152
Cardiologists, **5**:46
Cardiology
technicians, **1**:152
Cardiovascular
technicians, **2**:132
Career counselors, **1**:154
Career guidance
counselors, **2**:164,
2:166, **3**:92
Caretakers, **5**:88
Car painters, **1**:98
Carpenters, **1**:156. *See also*
Construction workers
Carpet layers, **3**:40

Car rental agents, **1**:158
Car repairers, **1**:88
Car sales. *See* Automobile
sales workers
Cartographers, **1**:160,
3:74. *See also* Surveyors
Cartographic
technicians, **6**:42
Cartoonists and
animators, **1**:162, **2**:38
Caseworkers, **6**:36
Cashiers, **1**:164
Cash-register
servicers, **4**:138
Casino workers, **3**:66
Casualty insurance
brokers, **5**:92
Caterers, **1**:166
Cement masons, **1**:168
Central office
operators, **6**:84
Central office
technicians, **6**:98
Ceramic engineers, **1**:170
Ceramics industry
workers, **5**:78
Certified public
accountants, **1**:12, **1**:84
Charitable
organizations, **3**:56
Chauffeurs, **5**:88. *See also*
Taxi drivers
Chauffeurs, **5**:88
Check-out clerks, **1**:164.
See also Counter and retail
clerks
Chefs, **2**:58. *See also*
Bakers; Cooks and Chefs
Chemical engineering
technicians, **1**:174
Chemical engineers, **1**:172,
5:18
Chemicals. *See* Industrial
chemical workers
Chemicals workers,
3:126
Chemical technicians, **1**:174
Chemists, **1**:176
Chief executive
officers, **3**:70
Childcare workers, **2**:8,
4:118
Child development, **3**:106
Chippers, **4**:168
Chiropractors, **2**:10

Choreographers, **2**:12, **2**:82
City managers, **2**:14
City planners, **2**:16
Civil engineering
technicians, **2**:18
Civil engineers, **1**:50, **2**:20,
3:90
Claims adjusters, **3**:152,
3:154
Claims clerks, **3**:152
Claims examiners, **3**:152
Cleaning people and
services, **3**:116, **3**:164,
5:88
Clergy. *See* Protestant
ministers; Rabbis; Roman
Catholic priests
Clerical supervisors and
managers, **2**:22
Clerks, **3**:24, **3**:72. *See also*
Counter and retail clerks
Clerk typists, **6**:136
Climate control
specialists, **2**:168
Climatologists, **4**:90
Clothing design, **3**:16
Clothing
manufacturing, **3**:174
Cloth manufacturing, **6**:108
Coaches, **1**:74, **6**:52
Coal mining
technicians, **2**:24
Coal mining workers, **2**:26
Coast Guard, **4**:94
Code administrators, **2**:50
Collection workers, **2**:28
College administrators, **2**:32
College admissions
directors, **2**:30
College and university
faculty, **1**:34, **1**:48, **1**:70,
2:34, **4**:62, **5**:70. *See also*
Biologists; Historians;
Linguists; Music teachers
College and university
financial aid officers, **2**:36
College deans and related
workers, **2**:34
College financial aid
administrators, **2**:36
Commercial and industrial
electronic equipment
repairers, **3**:130
Commercial artists, **1**:58,
2:38, **2**:102

Commercial decorators, **2**:116

Commodity traders, **6**:66. *See also* Grain merchants

Communications equipment mechanics, **2**:40

Community college teachers, **2**:34

Community service workers, **3**:122

Companions, **5**:88, 5:88. *See also* Housekeepers

Composers, **2**:42

Computer-aided drafting technicians, **1**:146

Computer-aided manufacturing technicians, **1**:146

Computer equipment repairers, **4**:138

Computer managers. *See* Data base managers

Computer operators, **2**:44, **5**:174

Computer programmers, **2**:46, **6**:86. *See also* Data base managers

Computer scientists. *See* Mathematicians; Systems analysts

Computer-service technicians, **2**:48

Computer systems, **3**:142

Concierges, **3**:116, **3**:120

Condominium managers, **5**:94

Conductors. *See* Orchestra conductors; Railroad conductors

Confectionery industry workers, **1**:148

Conservation, **1**:32

Conservationists, **5**:130

Construction. *See* Civil engineers

Construction inspectors, **2**:50

Construction machinery, **4**:140

Construction trades supervisors, **2**:52

Construction workers, **1**:60, **1**:138, **2**:54, **2**:130, **5**:54

Consular officers, **3**:48

Consultants, **4**:48

Contact lens manufacturing workers, **2**:56

Continuing education teachers. *See* Adult education teachers

Contractors, **1**:138, **1**:156, **2**:50, **2**:52, **2**:66, **2**:130, **3**:150, **4**:166, **5**:58, **5**:164. *See* Architectural technicians; Construction workers; Plumbers

Control technicians, **3**:138

Cooks and chefs, **2**:58, **5**:88

Copywriters, **2**:136

Coremakers, **2**:60

Correction officers, **2**:62

Cosmetologists, **2**:64

Cosmologists, **1**:70

Cost estimators, **2**:66

Costume making, **1**:14

Council-management government, **2**:14

Counselors. *See* Human services workers; Psychologists; Rehabilitation counselors; Therapists

Counter and retail clerks, **2**:67

Court reporters, **2**:70

Courts, **3**:168, **4**:14

Crane operators, **4**:140

Creative directors, **2**:72

Credit unions, **1**:26

Crime laboratory technologists, **2**:74

Criminal investigations, **3**:26

Crop production, **1**:32

Crop production technicians, **2**:176

Cryptographic technicians, **2**:76

Culinary arts. *See* Bakers; Cooks and chefs

Curators, **1**:54, **4**:110

Custodians, **3**:164

Customer service, **2**:67

Customs-house brokers, **2**:172

Customs inspectors, **3**:96

Dairy cattle. *See* Livestock management

Dairy farmers, **2**:78, **3**:10

Dairy products manufacturing workers, **2**:80

Dance directors, **2**:82

Dancers, **2**:82. *See also* Actors and actresses; Choreographers

Dance teachers, **2**:12

Dance therapists, **5**:138

Darkroom technicians, **2**:84, **5**:38

Data base managers, **2**:74, **2**:86. *See also* Medical records administrators

Data entry clerks, **2**:88

Data-processing technicians, **5**:174, **6**:164

Day-care workers, **2**:8, **5**:82

Day workers, **5**:88

Deaf interpreters, **3**:160

Dean of students, **2**:34

Debt collectors, **2**:28

Decorators, **3**:158

Deep-water diving and life-support technicians, **2**:118

Delivery drivers, **1**:104, **2**:90, **2**:128

Demographers, **2**:92

Demurrage clerks, **5**:126

Dental assistants, **2**:94

Dental ceramists, **2**:98

Dental hygienists, **2**:96

Dental-laboratory technicians, **2**:98

Dentists, **2**:100

Denture contour wire specialists, **2**:98

Departure controllers, **1**:38

Dermatologists, **5**:46. *See also* Electrologists

Designers, **1**:24, **2**:102. *See also* Industrial designers

Design technicians, **2**:126

Detectives, **5**:90, **6**:58

Developmental psychologists, **5**:104

Development officers, **3**:56

Diagnostic medicine, **6**:168

Dialysis technicians, **2**:104

Diesel mechanics, **2**:106

Dietetic technicians, **2**:108

Dietitians, **2**:110

Digester operators, **4**:168

Dippers, **5**:78

Director of housing, **2**:32

Director of religious activities, **2**:32

Director of student activities, **2**:32

Disabled people, **5**:146

Disc jockeys, **2**:112, **5**:120

Dispatcher. *See* Radio and telegraph operators

Dispatcher clerks, **5**:126

Dispensing opticians, **2**:114, **4**:146

Display workers, **2**:116

Diving technicians, **2**:118

Dock workers, **6**:64

Doctors. *See* Family practitioners; Physicians; Surgeons

Doctor's assistants, **5**:44

Dog groomers, **2**:120

Doorkeepers, **3**:118

Door-to-door sales workers, **2**:122

Dough mixers, **1**:104

Doughnut makers, **1**:104

Drafters, **2**:124, **2**:144

Drafting and design technicians, **2**:126

Draftsmen. *See* Drafting and design technicians

Drawing, **1**:58, **1**:162, **2**:124. *See* Architects; Artists; Cartoonists

Drive-in restaurants, **3**:18

Drivers, **1**:140, **6**:132

Drug abuse counselors, **3**:122

Druggists, **5**:28

Drug manufacturing, **5**:30

Dry cleaning and laundry workers, **2**:128

Drying machine operators, **5**:78

Drywall installers and finishers, **2**:130

Earth sciences, **3**:76, **3**:90, **5**:16

ECG technicians, **2**:132

Ecologists, **5**:130

183

Economic
 geographers, **3**:74
Economists, **2**:134
Editors, **2**:136. *See also*
 Technical writers; Writers
Educational media
 technicians, **1**:82
Education directors, **4**:110
EEG technicians, **2**:138
Efficiency experts, **3**:138
Elected officials, **5**:106
Electrical and electronics
 engineers, **2**:140
Electrical repairers, **2**:142
Electrical
 technicians, **2**:144, **2**:150
Electricians, **2**:146, **4**:30.
 See also Electrical
 repairers
Electric power maintenance
 technicians, **2**:168
Electric power
 workers, **2**:148
Electrocardiograph
 technicians, **2**:132
Electroencephalographic
 technicians, **2**:138
Electromechanical
 technicians, **2**:150
Electronic equipment, **1**:78
Electronic home
 entertainment equipment
 repairers, **3**:108
Electronic-organ
 technicians, **3**:108
Electronics, **1**:22, **1**:100,
 3:130, **3**:156, **5**:84
Electronics technicians,
 2:144, **2**:154
Electronics test
 technicians, **2**:154
Electron microscope, **1**:124
Electroplating
 workers, **2**:156
Elementary school
 teachers, **2**:158. *See also*
 Kindergarten teachers;
 Music teachers
Elevator installers and
 repairers, **2**:160
Embalmers, **3**:58
Embassies, **3**:48
Emergency medical
 technicians, **2**:162
Emissions technicians, **1**:96

Employment
 agencies, **2**:166
Employment agency
 workers, **1**:154
Employment
 counselors, **2**:164. *See
 also* Career counselors;
 Guidance counselors
Employment firm
 workers, **2**:166. *See also*
 Career counselors
EMTs. *See* Emergency
 medical technicians
Energy conservation
 and use technicians,
 2:168
Engineering, **1**:28. *See also*
 Biomedical Engineers; Civil
 engineers
Engineering
 technologists, **2**:168
Engineers, **1**:52, **1**:170,
 1:172. *See also* Aerospace
 engineers; Civil engineers;
 Locomotive engineers;
 Mining engineers;
 Operating engineers
Engravers, **5**:32
Enologist. *See* Winemakers
Environmental control
 specialists, **2**:168
Environmental
 designers, **2**:170, **4**:8
Environmental health
 inspectors, **3**:96
Environmental
 technicians, **5**:72
Equipment repairers,
 1:30, **3**:8, **3**:67, **3**:100,
 3:108, **3**:130, **4**:138,
 6:144
Ergonomists, **2**:170
Ethnologists, **1**:44
Etymologists, **4**:34
Executives, **3**:70
Executive search
 services, **2**:166
Export-import
 specialists, **2**:172
Express clerks, **5**:126
Extension work
 instructors, **2**:34
Exterminators, **5**:12
Eyeglasses, **2**:114. *See*
 Dispensing opticians

Fabricators, **5**:62
Factory designers, **3**:138
Factory machinery
 repair, **3**:148
Factory supervisor, **4**:54
Family nurse
 practitioners, **4**:130
Family practitioners, **2**:174,
 5:46
Family relations, **3**:106
Farm animals, **1**:42
Farm crop production
 technicians, **2**:176
Farm-equipment
 mechanics, **1**:28, **1**:30,
 3:8
Farmers, **1**:26, **2**:78, **3**:10.
 See also Agribusiness
 technicians; Agricultural
 extension service workers;
 Dairy farmers; Grain
 merchants
Farm operatives and
 managers, **3**:12
Farriers, **3**:14
Fashion designers, **3**:16
Fashion models, **4**:102
Fast food workers, **3**:18
FBI agents, **3**:20, **6**:12
Federal Aviation
 Administration, **1**:38
Federal Bureau of
 Investigation. *See* FBI
 agents
Field contractors, **5**:112
Field interviewers, **4**:60
Field technicians, **3**:22
Field work, **1**:44, **1**:48
Field workers, **5**:108
File clerks, **3**:24
Financial aid
 administrators, **2**:36
Financial management,
 1:12, **1**:26, **1**:32,
 1:84, **1**:108
Fine artists, **1**:58
Fingerprint classifiers, **3**:26
Fingerprints, **2**:74
Finishing workers, **4**:18
Firearms. *See* Gunsmiths
Fire control and safety
 technicians, **3**:28
Firefighters, **3**:28, **3**:30
Fire marshals, **3**:30
Firers, **4**:40, **5**:80

Fishers, commercial, **3**:32
Fish-production
 technicians, **3**:34
Fitters, **5**:54
Flight attendants, **3**:36
Flight engineers, **3**:38
Flood control, **1**:28
Floor assemblers, **1**:62
Floor covering
 installers, **3**:40
Floriculture workers, **4**:156
Fluid-power
 technicians, **3**:42
Flying. *See* Pilots
Food and drug inspectors,
 3:96
Food companies, **1**:26
Food inspection. *See* Health
 and regulatory
 inspectors
Food managers, **5**:154
Food manufacturing, **3**:34
Food manufacturing
 workers, **1**:150
Food preparation, **1**:166
Food production, **4**:64. *See*
 Canning and preserving
 industry workers
Food service
 management, **2**:108
Food service
 workers, **2**:58, **2**:110,
 3:44. *See also* Bakers;
 Cooks and chefs
Food technologists, **3**:46
Foot doctors, **5**:66
Foreign-service
 officers, **3**:48
Foreman, **4**:54
Foresters, **3**:50
Forest rangers, **5**:130
Forestry technicians, **3**:52,
 4:156
Forge shop workers, **3**:54
Fork-lift drivers, **3**:140
Foundations, **3**:56
Foundry workers, **2**:60,
 4:104
Freight rate analysts, **6**:128
Fumigators, **5**:12
Fundraisers, **3**:56, **6**:100
Funeral directors and
 embalmers, **3**:58. *See
 also* Mortuary science
 technicians

Furniture manufacturing
workers, **3**:60
Furniture movers, **3**:62
Furniture repair, **3**:64
Furniture
upholsterers, **3**:64
Future Farmers of
America, **1**:32

Gambling. *See* Gaming
occupations
Gaming occupations, **3**:66
Garbage collectors, **5**:142
Gardening. *See* Landscape
architects
Garment
industry workers, **3**:174
Gas burner mechanics, **3**:98
Gas drilling workers, **5**:166
Gas fitters, **5**:54
Gas station
attendants, **1**:90, **6**:20
Gate tenders, **6**:14
Gear workers, **6**:64
Gemologists. *See*
Jewelers
General maintenance
mechanics, **3**:67
General managers and top
executives, **3**:70
General office clerks, **3**:72
General practitioners, **5**:46
Geodetic technicians, **6**:42
Geographers, **3**:74. *See also*
Cartographers
Geologists, **3**:76, **3**:90. *See
also* Petroleum engineers
Geophysicists, **3**:78, **3**:90
Glass manufacturing
workers, **3**:80
Glaziers, **3**:82
Goldsmiths. *See*
Jewelers
Golf club assemblers, **6**:50
Government, **2**:14
Government aid
counselors, **3**:122
Government work, **2**:14.
See Foreign-Service
officers; Public office
holders
Governors, **5**:106
Grain buyers, **5**:112
Grain merchants, **3**:84

Grape growers. *See*
Winemakers
Graphic arts
technicians, **3**:86
Graphic
communications, **5**:86
Graphic designers, **2**:38,
2:102
Graphics
programmers, **3**:88
Greenhouses, **1**:34
Grocery store clerks, **2**:67
Grocery store
workers, **4**:66
Ground controllers, **1**:38
Grounds managers, **4**:103
Grounds
superintendents, **4**:10
Groundwater
professionals, **3**:90
Guidance
counselors, **1**:154, **3**:92.
See also Employment
counselors; Human
services workers
Gunsmiths, **3**:94
Gymnastics, **2**:82
Gynecologists, **5**:46

Hairstylists, **2**:64
Handicapped people, **5**:146
4-H Club, **1**:26, **1**:34
Headhunters. *See*
Employment firm workers
Headwaiters, **6**:150
Health aides, **3**:110
Health and regulatory
inspectors, **3**:96
Health care
administrators, **3**:112
Health care
workers, **6**:168. *See*
Dental hygienists; Hospital
attendants; Perfusionists;
Physicians as examples;
Registered nurses
Heart-lung machine
operators, **5**:8
Heart machines, **1**:152
Heating and cooling
mechanics, **3**:98
Heating and cooling
technicians, **3**:100
Heating specialists, **2**:168
Heating technicians, **3**:100

Heat treaters, **3**:102
Highway toll
collectors, **6**:118
Highway workers. *See* Toll
collectors
Historians, **3**:104
Hold workers, **6**:64
Home economists, **3**:106
Home electronic
repairers, **3**:108
Homemaker-home health
aides, **3**:110
Home management, **3**:106
Honey production, **1**:116
Horse shoers, **3**:14
Horticultural
therapists, **5**:138
Horticulturists, **1**:34
Hospital
administrators, **3**:112
Hospital attendants, **3**:114
Hot-cell technicians, **5**:40
Hotel and motel
management, **3**:116,
3:118
Hotel and motel
workers, **3**:118
Hotel clerks, **3**:120
Hot press operators, **5**:78
Hot tub servicers, **6**:82
Housekeepers, **3**:118, **5**:88
House sales, **5**:132
Human service
workers, **3**:122
Hydrogeologists, **3**:90
Hydrologists, **3**:78, **5**:22

Ice cream manufacturing
workers, **2**:80
Identification
technicians, **3**:124
Illustrators, **1**:58, **2**:38
Immigration
inspectors, **3**:96
Import specialists, **2**:172
Industrial chemical
workers, **3**:126
Industrial designers, **3**:128,
3:132
Industrial electronic
equipment
repairers, **3**:130
Industrial electronics
technicians, **3**:130

Industrial engineering
technicians, **3**:138
Industrial engineers, **3**:132
Industrial machinery
mechanics, **3**:134
Industrial-safety-and-health
technicians, **3**:138
Industrial traffic
managers, **3**:136
Industrial-truck
operators, **3**:140
Information clerks, **5**:134
Information scientists,
3:142, **4**:22, **6**:86
Information specialists, **4**:22
Inhalation therapists, **5**:152
Instructional design, **1**:82
Instrumentation
technicians, **3**:144
Instrument makers, **3**:146
Instrument repairers, **3**:148
Insulation workers, **3**:150
Insurance agencies, **1**:26
Insurance brokers, **4**:28
Insurance claims
representatives, **3**:152
Insurance companies, **5**:92,
6:140
Insurance policy processing
occupations, **3**:154
Integrated circuit
technicians, **3**:156
Interior designers and
decorators, **3**:158
Internists, **5**:46
Interpreters, **3**:160, **4**:34
Inventors. *See* Biomedical
engineers
Investigative workers. *See*
Polygraph examiners;
Private investigators
Investigators, **3**:124, **6**:58
Investment officers, **1**:108
Iron and steel industry
workers, **3**:162
Iron casting workers, **2**:60
Iron workers, **3**:54
Isotope-production
technicians, **5**:40

Janitors and cleaners, **3**:164
Jewelers, **3**:166. *See also*
Watch repairers
Jewelry repairers, **3**:166

185

Jigger operators, **5**:78
Journey workers, **5**:54
Judges, **3**:168

Keypunch operators, **2**:88
Kidney dialysis
  technicians, **2**:104
Kindergarten
  teachers, **3**:170
Kinesiotherapists, **3**:172
Kitchen helpers, **2**:58
Knit goods industry
  workers, **3**:174
Knitters, **3**:174

Laboratories, **1**:40, **1**:174,
  1:176, **2**:74
Laboratory
  technicians, **4**:78, **4**:84
Laboratory work. *See*
  Biologists; Chemists
Laborers, **2**:54
Labor relations
  specialists, **4**:166
Labor union business
  agents, **3**:176, **4**:166
Landscape architects, **4**:8
Landscape
  contractors, **4**:103
Landscapers and grounds
  managers, **4**:103
Land surveying, **6**:80
Land title searchers, **6**:114
Languages, **4**:34
Laser and laser test
  technicians, **4**:12
Laundry spotters, **2**:128
Law, **3**:168
Law enforcement
  workers, **3**:20, **5**:67
Lawn service
  specialists, **4**:10
Lawyers, **4**:14. *See also*
  Judges
Layout workers, **1**:132,
  4:16
Leather tanning and finishing
  workers, **4**:18
Legal assistants, **4**:20
Legal investigators, **5**:90
Legal secretaries, **6**:10
Letter carriers, **4**:46
Librarians, **4**:22

Library assistants, **1**:62,
  4:24. *See also* Bindery
  workers
Library technical
  assistants, **4**:24
Licensed practical
  nurses, **4**:26
Lie detector testers, **5**:74
Life insurance agents and
  brokers, **4**:28
Life scientists, **1**:126
Lights operators, **4**:30
Light technicians, **4**:30
Line installers, **2**:148
Line mechanics, **1**:36
Linesmen, **6**:138
Linguists, **4**:34
Lithographic workers, **4**:36
Livery. *See* Taxi
  drivers
Livestock management,
  1:32
Load dispatcher, **2**:148
Lobbyists, **5**:110
Locksmiths, **4**:38
Locomotive engineers, **4**:40
Loggers, **5**:170
Logging industry
  workers, **4**:42
Longshore workers, **6**:64
Lotteries. *See* Gaming
  occupations
Lumberyard workers, **5**:170

Macaroni products industry
  workers, **4**:174
Machine movers, **6**:70
Machine repair, **1**:46
Machinery, **3**:134
Machinery design, **3**:128
Machinery erectors, **4**:96
Machinery operators, **1**:30,
  1:90, **4**:140
Machinery repair, **4**:96
Machinists, **4**:16, **4**:44. *See
  also* Millwrights; Tool and
  die makers
Mail carriers, **4**:46
Maintenance
  electricians, **2**:142
Management analysts and
  consultants, **4**:48
Management trainees, **4**:50
Managers, **1**:26, **1**:66, **3**:70

Manual-arts
  therapists, **5**:138
Manufacturers' sales
  representatives, **4**:52
Manufacturing, **3**:100,
  5:114, **6**:108
Manufacturing metal, **3**:102
Manufacturing trades
  supervisor, **4**:54
Mapmakers, **1**:160, **3**:74,
  6:78
Mapping technicians, **6**:78
Marble setters, tile setters,
  and terrazzo
  workers, **4**:56
Marine engineers, **4**:58
Marine geologists, **3**:76
Marines, **4**:94
Marketing, **6**:100
Marketing executives, **4**:52,
  6:18
Marketing
  researchers, **4**:60
Masons, **1**:168. *See*
  Bricklayers and
  stonemasons
Mathematical skills, **1**:12
Mathematicians, **1**:16, **4**:62
Mayors, **5**:106
Measuring devices, **3**:146
Meatcutters, **4**:66
Meat inspectors, **6**:146
Meat-packing production
  workers, **4**:64
Meat packing
  workers, **4**:64
Mechanical engineers, **4**:68
Mechanical equipment, **1**:22
Mechanical
  technicians, **4**:70
Mechanics, **3**:134, **4**:100.
  See also Automobile
  mechanics
Media assistants, **4**:72
Media director, **4**:72
Media directors, **4**:72
Media planners and
  buyers, **4**:72
Media specialists (school),
  4:74
Mediators, **3**:176
Medical assistants, **4**:76
Medical instruments, **1**:130
Medical-laboratory
  technicians, **4**:78

Medical records
  administrators, **4**:80
Medical records
  technicians, **4**:82
Medical secretaries, **6**:10
Medical technologists, **4**:84
Medicine, **1**:124, **1**:176.
  See Biomedical Engineers;
  Biomedical equipment
  technicians; Chiropractors;
  Hospital administrators;
  Physicians; Veterinarians
Membership
  secretaries, **6**:10
Mental health
  workers, **5**:102
Mental hospital
  workers, **4**:132
Merchandising, **1**:142
Merchant marine
  workers, **4**:86
Metallographers, **4**:88
Metallurgical
  technicians, **4**:88
Metal products, **3**:102
Metals engineers, **4**:88
Metal workers, **3**:54, **6**:30.
  See also Patternmakers
Meteorological
  technicians, **6**:42
Meteorologists, **3**:78, **4**:90
Meter readers, **4**:92
Methods-engineering
  technicians, **3**:138
Microchips, **3**:156, **5**:84
Microelectronics
  technicians, **6**:16
Microphones, **1**:78
Microwave
  technicians, **6**:98
Military careers, **4**:94
Military training, **1**:22
Military training and
  service, **1**:38, **1**:70
Milking machine
  systems, **1**:30
Milk products
  manufacturing, **2**:80
Millwrights, **4**:96, **5**:170
Mineralogists, **5**:22
Miners, **2**:26
Mining engineers, **4**:98
Mobile heavy equipment
  mechanics, **4**:100
Model dressers, **2**:116

Models, **4**:102
Molders, **4**:104. *See also* Coremakers
Molding plasterers, **5**:58
Mold workers, **3**:162
Money, **1**:12
Mortgage lenders, **1**:64, **1**:108
Morticians, **3**:58
Mortuary science technicians, **3**:58
Motel management. *See* Hotel and motel management
Motion picture photographers, **5**:34
Motion picture projectionists, **4**:106
Motion pictures, **1**:14
Motion picture theater workers, **4**:106
Motorcycle mechanics, **4**:108
Motor vehicle emissions technicians, **1**:96
Motor vehicle inspectors, **3**:96
Movers. *See* Furniture movers
Moving van drivers, **3**:62
Municipal government, **2**:14
Museum professionals, **4**:110
Museum technicians, **4**:110
Museum workers, **1**:44, **1**:48, **1**:58
Musical instrument repairers, **4**:112, **5**:56. *See also* Pipe organ technicians
Music composition, **2**:42
Musicians, **4**:114. *See also* Orchestra Conductors; Singers
Music industry, **2**:112
Music teachers, **4**:116
Music therapists, **5**:138

Nannies, **4**:118
Natural gas drilling, **5**:14
Naval architecture, **4**:58
Navy, **4**:94
Nephrology, **2**:104
Network control technicians, **6**:98

Newscasters, **5**:122
Newswriters, **6**:6:166
Not-for-profit organizations, **3**:56
Nuclear engineers, **4**:120
Nuclear instrumentation technicians, **4**:122
Nuclear medicine technologists, **4**:124
Nuclear power plants, **2**:168
Nuclear reactor operator technicians, **4**:126
Nurse anesthetists, **4**:128
Nurse practitioners, **4**:130
Nursery school teachers, **2**:8, **5**:82
Nursery workers, **4**:156
Nurses. *See* Licensed practical nurses; Nurse practitioners; Physician's assistants; Registered nurses
Nursing and psychiatric aides, **4**:132
Nursing home workers, **4**:132, **5**:100
Nutrition, **1**:124, **3**:106
Nutritionists, **2**:108, **2**:110

Obstetricians, **5**:46
Occupational-safety-and-health inspectors, **3**:96
Occupational therapists, **4**:134
Oceanographers, **4**:136
Office-machine servicers, **4**:138
Office workers, **3**:24, **3**:72
Oil burner mechanics, **3**:98
Oil drilling engineers, **5**:16
Oil drilling occupations, **5**:14, **5**:20
Oil refineries, **5**:18
Oil rig workers, **5**:166
Opera singers, **6**:32
Operating engineers, **4**:140
Operations-research analysts, **4**:142
Operators. *See* Telephone operators
Ophthalmic laboratory technicians, **4**:144
Optical mechanics, **4**:146

Opticians, **2**:114
Optics technicians, **4**:148
Optomechanical technicians, **4**:148
Optometric technicians, **4**:150
Optometrists, **4**:146, **4**:152
Oral pathologists, **2**:100
Oral surgeons, **2**:100
Orchestra conductors, **4**:154
Orderlies, **3**:114
Organizational development, **4**:48
Organizations. *See* General managers and top executives
Ornamental horticulture technicians, **4**:156
Orthodontics technicians, **2**:98
Orthodontists, **2**:100
Orthotists, **5**:96
Osteopathic physicians, **4**:158
Outdoor work, **3**:32
Overhaul mechanics, **1**:36
Oxidizers, **6**:30

Packaging and paper products technicians, **4**:160
Packaging engineers, **4**:162
Packaging technicians, **4**:160
Paint and coatings industry workers, **4**:164
Painters and paperhangers, **4**:166. *See also* Artists; Automotive painters
Paint industry workers, **4**:164
Painting. *See also* Automotive painters
Paleontologists, **3**:76
Papermaking occupations, **4**:168
Paper products technicians, **4**:160
Paralegals, **4**:20
Paramedics, **2**:162
Park design. *See* Landscape architects
Park rangers, **3**:50, **4**:170.

See also Forestry technicians
Park technicians, **4**:172
Party planning, **1**:166
Pasta makers, **4**:174
Pathologists, **6**:48
Patternmakers, **4**:176
Pavers, **1**:60
PBX installers, **6**:102
PBX operators, **6**:84, **6**:104
PBX systems technicians, **6**:98
Pediatricians, **5**:46
Pedodontists, **2**:100
Pedontists, **2**:100
Perfusionists, **5**:8
Periodontists, **2**:100
Personnel and labor relations specialists, **5**:10
Personnel counselors, **2**:166
Personnel recruiters, **2**:166
Pest control workers, **5**:12
Petroleum drilling occupations, **5**:14
Petroleum engineers, **5**:16
Petroleum geologists, **3**:76
Petroleum refining workers, **5**:18
Petroleum technicians, **5**:20
Petrologists, **5**:22
Pet store workers, **2**:120
Pharmaceutical industry workers, **1**:174, **5**:24
Pharmaceutical technicians, **5**:26
Pharmacists, **5**:28
Pharmacologists, **1**:126, **5**:30. *See also* Toxicologists
Philologists, **4**:34
Photocopy machine repair, **4**:138
Photoengravers, **5**:32
Photographers, **5**:34
Photographer's assistants, **2**:84
Photographic equipment technicians, **5**:36
Photography, **1**:82
Photography developers, **2**:84
Photojournalists, **5**:34
Photo lab workers, **5**:38

Photomicroscope, 4:88
Photo-optics
 technicians, 4:148
Photo technicians, 5:84
Physical
 anthropologists, 1:44
Physical radiological
 technicians, 5:40
Physical therapists, 5:42.
 See also Kinesiotherapists;
 Rehabilitation counselors
Physicians, 2:174, 5:46.
 See also Family
 practitioners; Osteopathic
 physicians; Surgeons
Physician's assistants, 5:44
Physicists, 5:48
Piano technicians, 5:50
Pier superintendents, 6:64
Pilots, 5:52. *See also* Air
 traffic controllers; Flight
 attendants; Flight
 engineers
Pipefitters and
 steamfitters, 5:54
Pipe organ
 technicians, 5:56
Planes. *See*
 Airplanes
Planetary astronomers,
 1:70
Planners. *See* Architects;
 City planners
Plant engineers, 2:168,
 4:68
Plant-layout
 technicians, 3:138
Plants. *See* Agricultural
 scientists; Landscape
 architects
Plasterers, 5:58
Plastics engineers, 4:162
Plastics products
 manufacturing
 workers, 5:60
Plastics technicians, 5:62
Platemakers, 3:86
Playgrounds. *See* Landscape
 architects
Playwrights, 6:6:166
Plumbers, 5:64
Podiatrists, 5:66
Poisonous substance
 experts, 6:124
Police officers, 5:67

Police work, 3:20. *See also*
 Crime laboratory
 technologists; Polygraph
 examiners
Political scientists, 5:70
Politicians, 5:106
Pollution-control
 technicians, 1:32, 5:72
Polygraph examiners, 5:74
Population consultants, 2:92
Porcelain industry
 workers, 5:78
Postal clerks, 5:76
Postal service
 workers, 4:46
Pottery and porcelain
 industry workers, 5:78
Poultry dressers, 4:64
Poultry management, 1:34
Power plant
 operators, 4:126
Power plant workers, 5:80
Practical nurses, 4:26
Precision-lens
 technicians, 4:148
Prepress workers, 5:32
Preschool teachers, 3:170,
 5:82
Preservation
 workers, 4:110
Preserving industry
 workers, 1:150
Pressers or finishers, 2:128
Press operators, 5:86
Press secretaries, 5:110
Pretzel twisters, 1:104
Priests, 5:162
Principals, 5:172
Printed-circuit-board
 technicians, 5:84
Printers, 4:36, 6:134. *See
 also* Bindery workers
Printmakers, 5:32
Prison guards, 2:62
Private detectives, 6:12
Private household
 workers, 5:88
Private investigators,
 3:124, 5:90, 6:58.
 See also FBI agents
Procurement
 engineers, 5:112
Producers, 5:136
Product
 development, 1:176

Production machine
 operators, 4:44
Programmers (computer),
 2:46, 3:142
Property and casualty
 insurance agents and
 brokers, 5:92
Property and real estate
 managers, 5:94
Prosthetists and
 orthotists, 5:96
Protective service
 workers, 6:12
Protestant ministers, 5:98
Psychiatric aides, 4:132
Psychiatric social
 workers, 6:36
Psychiatric
 technicians, 5:100
Psychiatrists, 5:102
Psychological testing
 technicians, 6:106
Psychologists, 5:102,
 5:104
Public administration, 2:14,
 3:70
Public office holders, 5:106
Public opinion
 researchers, 5:108
Public relations
 specialists, 5:110
Publishing. *See* Editors;
 Graphic arts technicians;
 Typesetters;
 Writers
Purchasing agents, 5:112

Quality-control
 technicians, 3:138,
 5:114, 6:112
Quartermasters, 4:86

Rabbis, 5:116
Racetracks, 1:40, 3:14
Radar equipment, 1:38
Radiation technicians, 5:40
Radio, television, and print
 advertising sales
 workers, 1:20
Radio and telegraph
 operators, 5:118

Radio and television
 announcers, 5:120
Radio and television
 newscasters, 5:122
Radio and television program
 directors, 5:124
Radiographers, 5:40
Radiologists, 6:168
Radiology, 4:124
Radio station
 announcers, 2:112
Radio stations, 1:78
Radio station
 technicians, 6:44
Radio technicians, 3:22
Railroad clerks, 5:126
Railroad conductors, 5:128
Railroad crew
 workers, 4:40, 5:128
Railroad workers, 1:136
Range
 conservationists, 6:42
Range managers, 5:130
Rangers. *See* Park
 rangers
Rate supervisors, 6:128
Real estate agents and
 brokers, 1:64, 5:132
Real estate
 auctioneers, 1:76
Real estate managers,
 5:94
Receiving clerks, 6:24,
 6:68
Receptionists, 5:134
Recording industry
 workers, 5:136
Recording studios, 1:82
Recreational
 therapists, 5:138
Recreation areas. *See*
 Landscape architects
Recreation workers, 5:140
Recycling, 5:176
Recycling collectors, 5:142
Referees, 6:138
Refineries, 5:18
Refrigeration
 technicians, 3:100
Refrigeration
 mechanics, 3:98
Refrigerator repairers,
 1:46
Refuse collectors, 5:142
Registered nurses, 5:144

188

Registrars, 2:32
Rehabilitation
    counselors, 5:146. See
    also Recreational therapists
Rehabilitation therapists,
    3:172, 4:134, 5:42
Rental cars, 1:158
Rental property
    managers, 5:94
Research, 1:22, 2:34
Research associates, 4:110
Reservation and
    transportation ticket
    agents, 5:150
Reservation clerks, 3:120
Residence counselors, 2:32
Resort workers, 6:34
Respiratory
    therapists, 5:152
Restaurant managers, 5:154
Restaurant workers, 1:114,
    2:58, 3:18. See also Fast
    food workers
Retail sales
    workers, 1:142, 2:67,
    2:172, 5:156
Retail store
    managers, 5:158
Riding stables, 3:14
Riggers, 6:70
Road building
    machinery, 4:140
Roads, 1:60
Robotic technicians, 5:160
Robots. See Robotic
    technicians
Roman Catholic priests,
    5:162
Roof applicators, 5:164
Roofers, 5:164
Roustabouts, 5:166
Route-sales workers, 1:104
Rubber goods production
    workers, 5:168

Safety engineers, 3:28
Safety regulations, 3:96
Sailors, 4:86
Sales clerks, 1:164, 2:67,
    5:156
Sales executives, 1:20
Salespeople, 2:67
Sales representatives, 2:122,
    4:52, 6:18
Sales route drivers, 2:128

Sawmill workers, 5:170
School administrators,
    5:172
School guidance
    counselors, 3:92
School librarians, 4:74
School psychologists, 5:104
School secretaries, 6:10
School teachers. See
    Elementary school
    teachers; Preschool
    teachers; Secondary school
    teachers
Science, 1:26
Scientific and business data-
    processing
    technicians, 5:174
Scientific instruments,
    3:146
Scientific photographers,
    5:34
Scientists, 1:28, 1:34,
    1:70, 1:124, 1:176. See
    Agricultural scientists;
    Biologists; Chemists;
    Geologists; Physicists
Scorers, 6:138
Scrap metal processing
    workers, 5:176
Screenwriters, 6:166
Scuba divers, 2:118
Sculpture, 1:58
Secondary school
    teachers, 6:8
Secretarial
    supervisors, 2:22
Secretaries, 6:10, 6:136
Securities sales
    workers, 6:66
Security consultants, 6:12
Security guards, 6:14
Seismologists, 3:78
Semiconductor
    technicians, 6:16
Senators, 5:106
Separators, 5:32
Service employees, 3:164
Services sales
    representatives, 6:18
Service station
    attendants, 6:20
Service technicians, 3:108
Sewage plant
    operators, 6:154
Sewing. See Fashion

designers; Furniture
    upholsterers
Sheet-metal workers, 6:22
Sheriff officers. See Police
    officers
Shipbuilding, 1:132, 4:58
Shipping and receiving
    clerks, 6:24
Shipping clerks, 3:136
Shipping services sales
    representatives, 6:128
Ship runners, 6:24
Shoe industry
    workers, 6:26
Shoe repairers, 6:26, 6:28
Shopkeepers, 5:158
Shorthand reporters, 2:70,
    6:62
Short-order cooks, 3:18
Silverplaters, 2:156
Silversmiths, 6:30. See also
    Jewelers
Silverware industry
    workers, 6:30
Singers, 1:14, 6:32
Site bosses, 2:52
Ski lift operators, 6:34
Small appliance
    repairers, 1:46
Small engine
    repairers, 4:108
Snack-bar workers, 3:18
Social psychologists,
    5:104
Social scientists, 2:92,
    2:134, 5:108, 6:38
Social secretaries, 6:10
Social service agency
    workers, 3:122
Social workers, 6:36. See
    also Human service
    workers
Sociologists, 6:38
Soft-tool technicians, 5:84
Soil-conservation
    technicians, 6:42
Soil erosion, 1:28
Soil scientists, 6:40
Solar astronomers, 1:70
Sound equipment, 1:78
Sound mixers, 6:72
Sound-recording
    technicians, 1:78, 5:136,
    6:44
Sound technicians, 6:46

Space administration (NASA),
    1:70
Spacecraft, 1:22
Spacecraft repair, 1:100
Space design. See Architects
Space exploration, 1:24,
    1:68. See also Astronomers
Spa workers, 6:82
Spectrographic
    technicians, 4:88
Speech-language
    pathologists, 6:48
Speech technicians, 1:80
Sporting goods production
    workers, 6:50
Sports, 1:72, 1:74
Sportscasters, 5:120
Sports coaches, 6:52
Sports medicine. See Athletic
    trainers
Sprinkler fitters, 5:54
Stage production
    workers, 6:54
Stage technicians, 6:56
State police officers, 6:58
Statistical clerks, 6:60
Statisticians, 1:16, 2:92
Steel industry
    workers, 3:162
Stellar astronomers, 1:70
Stenographers, 6:62
Stevedores, 6:64
Stewards and
    stewardesses, 3:36
Stockbrokers, 1:108, 6:66
Stock clerks, 6:68
Stonemasons, 1:138
Store clerks, 2:67
Store managers, 5:158
Stove repairers, 1:46
Stove tenders, 3:162
Structural-steel
    workers, 6:70
Stucco masons, 5:58
Studio technicians, 6:72
Submarine cable equipment
    technicians, 6:98
Substation operator, 2:148
Superintendents, 5:172
Surgeons, 5:46, 6:74
Surgery, animals, 1:40
Surgical technicians, 6:76
Surveying and mapping
    technicians, 6:78. See
    also Cartographers

Surveyors, **6:**80

Swimming-pool servicers, **6:**82

Switchboard operators, **6:**84

Switchboard operators, **5:**80

Switching equipment technicians, **6:**98

Symphony orchestra members, **4:**114

Systems analysts, **6:**86. *See also* Information scientists

Systems programmers, **2:**46

Tape recorders, **1:**78

Taxidermists, **6:**88

Taxi drivers, **6:**90

Tax preparers, **6:**92

Tax returns, **1:**12

Teacher aides, **6:**94

Teachers. *See* Adult and vocational education teachers; Agricultural extension service workers; College and university faculty; Elementary school teachers; Preschool teachers; Secondary school teachers

Teaching. *See* Adult and vocational education teachers; College and university faculty

Teamsters. *See* Delivery drivers; Truck drivers

Technical writers, **6:**96

Technology, **1:**26

Teeth-cleaning, **2:**96

Telecommunications technicians, **6:**98

Telegraph operators, **5:**118

Telemarketing, **6:**100

Telephone equipment installers, **2:**40

Telephone installers and repairers, **6:**102

Telephone operators, **6:**84, **6:**104

Telescopes, **1:**70

Television, **1:**14. *See also* Cartoonists

Television announcers, **5:**120

Television cartoons, **1:**162

Television newscasters, **5:**122

Television production technicians, **4:**30

Television programming, **1:**14

Television stations, **1:**78

Television studio technicians, **1:**78, **3:**22, **6:**44

Television studio workers, **6:**72

Tellers, **1:**106, **1:**110

Termite exterminators, **5:**12

Terrazzo workers, **4:**56

Testing technicians, **6:**106

Textile technicians, **6:**108

Textile workers, **6:**110. *See also* Knit goods industry workers

Theater managers, **4:**106

Theatre workers, **1:**14, **6:**54, **6:**56

Therapists, **5:**102, **5:**104, **5:**138, **6:**36. *See also* Human services workers; Psychiatrists; Psychologist; Psychologists; Rehabilitation counselors

Ticket agents, **5:**150

Ticket sellers, **1:**164

Ticket takers, **4:**106

Tilers, **3:**40

Tile setters, **4:**56

Tire technicians, **6:**112

Title searchers and examiners, **6:**114

Tobacco products industry workers, **6:**116

Toll collectors, **6:**118

Tool and die makers, **6:**30, **6:**120

Tool design, **1:**22

Tool makers, **5:**62, **6:**120

Tools, **1:**30, 120

Tour guides, **6:**122

Tourist industry, **5:**150, **6:**122, **6:**130. *See also* Hotel and motel management

Tow truck drivers, **6:**20

Toxicologists, **1:**176, **6:**124

Toy industry workers, **6:**126

Traffic agents and clerks, **6:**128

Traffic managers, **6:**128. *See also* Industrial traffic managers

Train clerks, **5:**126

Trainers. *See* Athletic trainers

Trains, **4:**40

Transcribing machine operators, **6:**136

Translators, **3:**160. *See also* Linguists

Transportation inspectors, **3:**96

Transportation workers, **1:**136, **2:**90, **5:**126

Travel. *See* Flight attendants

Travel agents, **5:**150, **6:**130. *See also* Reservation and transportation ticket agents

Tree planters, **3:**52

Trouble shooters, **2:**148

Truck drivers, **2:**90, **5:**142, **6:**132. *See also* Moving van drivers

Truckers, **3:**140

Turbine operators, **5:**80

Tutoring. *See* Teachers

Typesetters, **6:**134

Typewriter repairers, **4:**138

Typists, **6:**62, **6:**136, **6:**164

Umpires, **6:**138

Underwriters, **6:**140

University admissions directors, **2:**30

University faculty, **2:**34

Upholsterers, **3:**64

Urban anthropologists, **1:**44

Urban geographers, **3:**74

Urban planners, **2:**16

U.S. Government. *See* Foreign-service officers; Public office holders

Used car dealers, **1:**98

Ushers, **4:**106, **6:**142

Utility company employees, **2:**148

Utility company workers, **2:**148, **4:**92, **5:**80

Utility plant operators, **4:**126

Utilization engineers, **4:**68

Vault workers, **6:**24

VDT operators, **6:**154

Vehicle repair, **1:**90

Vending machine mechanics, **6:**144

Verifier operators, **2:**88

Veterans' coordinators, **2:**32

Veterinarians, **6:**146. *See also* Animal health technicians; Farriers

Video technicians, **6:**148

Vintners, **6:**160

Visiting nurses, **3:**110

Vocational education. *See* Adult and vocational education teachers

Vocational training instructors, **1:**18

Voluntary organizations, **3:**56

Waiters and waitresses, **6:**150. *See also* Fast food workers

Wallpaper hangers, **4:**166

Washing machine operators, **2:**128

Washing machine repairers, **1:**46

Waste management, **5:**142

Watch repairers, **6:**152

Water and wastewater treatment-plant operators, **6:**154

Water pollution-control technicians, **5:**72

Weapons dealers, **3:**94

Weathermen, **4:**90

Welders, **6:**156

Welding technicians, **6:**156

Wholesale buying, **1:**142; **6:**158

Wholesalers, **2:**172; **6:**158

Wholesale sales workers, **6:**158

Wildlife workers, **3**:52
Winch operators, **6**:64
Window display
  workers, **2**:116
Winemakers, **6**:160
Wood machinists, **3**:60
Wood products
  technicians, **6**:162

Wood science and technology
  careers, **6**:162
Wood scientists, **6**:162
Wood technologists, **6**:162
Woodworkers, **1**:156, **3**:60,
  4:176
Woodworking, **4**:176. *See*
  Gunsmiths

Word processor
  operators, **6**:136, **6**:164
Work environment
  design, **2**:170
Work-measurement
  technicians, **3**:138
Writers, **1**:86;**6**:166, **3**:104.
  See also Editors;

Historians; Linguists;
Technical writers

X-ray technologists, **2**:10;
  4:90;**6**:168

Yard clerks, **5**:126

Zoos, **1**:34, **1**:40